THE ONLY WAY

THE ONLY WAY

How Can the Germans Be Cured?

BY
KARL BARTH

PHILOSOPHICAL LIBRARY
New York

COPYRIGHT, 1947, BY
PHILOSOPHICAL LIBRARY, INC.
15 EAST 40TH STREET, NEW YORK 16, N. Y.

ISBN: 978-0-8065-2979-0

The first section, "How Can the Germans be Cured?" was translated by Marta K. Neufeld; the second section, "The Germans and Ourselves," by Ronald Gregor Smith.

PRINTED IN THE UNITED STATES OF AMERICA

Foreword

My lecture "The Germans and Ourselves" had a resounding *repercussion*, when given in January and February 1945, and later when published. I think of the reports in the Swiss press and I think even more of the many hopeful and hopeless letters I received during those last months. All this and the constantly deteriorating situation in Germany made me aware of the necessity of continuing to speak up.

The first article in this booklet was written at the request of the *Manchester Evening News.*

The two letters have been published with the kind permission of their German authors. The reason I used them for this aim, as related to the problem presented in the first part, is that these two letters indicate two German trends, both laid down in a noteworthy, original and impressive way and that they offered me the opportunity to answer directly or indirectly, completely or at least superficially, questions which have reached me from other quarters. My correspondents and I cannot really be blamed since today no one is in

FOREWORD

a position to come out with a definite solution. *Dies diem docebit!* A discussion proposing a possible solution can therefore profit the audience. It is obvious that in order to avoid any complications in the future, I cautiously omitted the names and addresses of my correspondents, the exact dates of their letters and mine, as well as all details which might give a hint as to their identity. On the other hand, I intentionally included the short exhortation concerning the "Movement for a Free Germany" at the end of my answer to the second letter, because I meant to stimulate the active participation of the German readers of this booklet in favor of the Movement, and the favorable attention of the Swiss readers.

I wanted others to participate in the task of encouraging the Germans to follow the path now open to them.

Basel,   K. B.
Switzerland.

Contents

Foreword	v
How Can the Germans Be Cured?	3
Letters	21
The Germans and Ourselves	63

How Can the Germans Be Cured?

Man has always been ill and always will be. In the life of individuals and nations, to be cured means: to become a little less ill. The general ill which afflicts humanity is today more visible than at any other time. But, even in the great hospital of the present some patients suffer from more serious diseases than others. And although many and important things concerning all the patients can be said towards the solution of this problem, it is true, nevertheless, that this problem, the problem of a certain cure, is to be considered and answered in different ways, according to each individual case. Among all the others, the German people seem to be the most seriously ill. It is therefore pertinent to ask oneself: how can the Germans be cured—that is, become a little bit less ill? Out of the many things which can be said, I shall choose only those of the utmost importance.

If confronted with this question one year ago, my first reaction would have been: all the Ger-

THE ONLY WAY

mans need for their political, moral and spiritual cure—on which everything depends—is the realization that their "Watch on the Rhine" has failed; the realization that their armies have been defeated on the battle-field, not only by the Russians, but, at last, also by the Western democracies whose military strength they so terribly despised. Above all, the collapse of their belief in their superior and unsurpassed military might—so dangerous for others and themselves—should be brought home to them once and for all. In my opinion, this obviously primary condition is fundamental. As long as the Germans are not deprived of their confidence in their military power by completely and ostentatiously taking it away from them, just as matches and knife are completely and ostentatiously taken away from a naughty child, there can be no question of German cure. For they suffered from this very military power and their confidence in it, for centuries, more than any other nation. But this condition—I am writing this on April 8, 1945—is about to be fulfilled and therefore does not necessitate any further emphasis.

A second necessity, which constantly gains in importance, is the following: Today, as larger and larger German territories fall under British, American and French control, all will depend on the

THE ONLY WAY

way in which the victors—owing to the Russian enigma, I refer only to the Western victors—will exercise their authority in Germany, so that the conduct of their armies, their civil servants and judiciary officials; the steps taken for the maintenance of order and progressive reestablishment of communications, administration, schools and churches, social and cultural organizations will constitute a practical lesson of that which is understood outside of Germany and especially in the West, under the names democracy, freedom, loyalty, humane conduct, wisdom, fair play, *savoir vivre* and as human justice and strength. The fact that the great majority of Germans have known—as far back as they can think—all these only in the form of clumsy German imitation or in the hostile distortion of German propaganda. The moment has come for them to see these things on the impressive background of the military victory of the nations standing for these ideas and to try these things in Germany. Neither the annihilation of the Nazi system and Prussian militarism nor any well-meaning theoretical counter-propaganda could help the Germans and do away with the German danger if the Allied regimes as such, the Allied governing and administrative skill; and if the foreign nations cannot prove beyond doubt that there

THE ONLY WAY

was and is outside of Germany something better than the politics, the methods, the way of life, the way of thinking and speaking which they considered until now the only possible and healthy ones. The Allies must succeed in the very things in which the Germans never and nowhere succeeded in the territories they occupied. After crushing the Germans, the Allies must succeed in convincing them that the Allied cause is a good one, to make them willing and eager and to stimulate them to proceed on a new path for themselves. Show them how gentlemen behave when they are in power! The Germans, or at least a majority of the people, are now ready to look for something better—there is no doubt about it—, and, for the time being, such a thing can be shown to them only by the victorious foreigners and not by other Germans. But they have to see it at work. I do not know how they can be cured, if the Allies miss this unique opportunity of teaching them this practical lesson.

The third responsibility of the Allies is the following: In the organization of the administration of occupied German territories, the Germans should be made to share responsibility of maintaining order in their public life, as soon as possible. The Germans are used to being ruled in this or in that way, from a central point within a hierarchy

THE ONLY WAY

and to obey any word or command coming from no matter how far. This is one of the traits because of which they suffered for centuries and which became deadly 12 years ago—and from which they must now be freed, whatever the price. Each of them must now learn to think for himself, of "community" and "state" in terms of his own political task and duty, instead of waiting for the command of a third person. The fact that individual responsibility for political situations is alien to them explains why it is so difficult to make them understand that they cannot simply be cleared of all charges brought against the Nazi system and all its consequences, but that they must be held responsible for all that has been done to them and to the rest of Europe. The education leading to such an admission can also be achieved only by direct practical teaching; they must be led at last, to take their public affairs soberly into their own hands and shape their future themselves in a common effort, so that all may be made to answer for the result of their enterprise.

There is really no hurry for the election of a German Parliament, nor for the establishment of a Central Government. It does not even matter much whether there will be, in the future, a unified German State, or whether the various states will be given again a relative independence. And it really does not matter much either to what extent German populations and territories will belong, in the future, to other, non-German countries. The idea of national unity within a state came on earth in the 19th century, from Hell rather than Heaven; it does not seem, anyhow, to have suited the Germans at all. The condition *sine qua non* for the German cure is that the German people, whether under their own sovereignty, or otherwise, be given political freedom; that is, the possibility of learning to be responsible for their own thinking and acting, as it can be done in the small and smallest circles, those small and smallest circles where it is practiced and learned with the best of results. The Allies should impose this task upon the Germans as soon as possible. And I emphasize the word impose. According to their old tradition, the Germans expect to be crushed under the heel of their new masters. And this will have to be so, as long as the reality and danger of National Socialism is not completely wiped out. The most powerful oppression to be inflicted upon the German people would be the one they least expect. It should consist in their being compelled to freedom, in their being called upon to advise and help themselves and to decide upon the men and women most worthy of their confidence and the new forms and essence of their political, social, economic, cultural and church life, in their local and central government, within the framework of legality and on behalf of the occupation forces. They should be given the compelling opportunity of shaping future history as their own history, instead of waiting to be driven by and for some collective power, instead of being carried along by mere chance or of being led anywhere by tradition or by the whims of a ruling class. They should be given the opportunity of becoming citizens, after having been officers or soldiers for so long! But this opportunity should be given to them in a way that would make its refusal impossible! And it should be given to them soon! Everything else can wait or be taken care of in some other way. The conversion to freedom, however, should not suffer any delay! The unliberated German will always be the diseased, the dangerous German. All depends on the Allies recognizing the urgency of this matter.

There are, of course, other conditions for the cure of the German people, which can be fulfilled only by the Germans themselves. It might, however, be useful and necessary for the others to realize what changes concerning the Germans must be made at all costs.

THE ONLY WAY

It is absolutely necessary that they should realize in the future, and for a long time, consider their own responsibility for their guilt in the past, as well as the task that lies ahead. The German thought has the fatal tendency of pointing to the actions of other people, of emphasizing the guilt of their accomplices, especially the guilt of outsiders and of expecting the confession and reprisals of others, when their most pertinent thoughts should be the ones concerning their own actions. It is obviously true that today all is not only German responsibility, guilt and task. The Germans should, however, have the grace to admit that today the responsibility of others does not concern them in the least. They should have the grace of not thinking today in terms of Europe or the globe, but merely in terms of Germany. And that, because it should be clear even to them that the German way of dealing for the last 12—one could even say 76—years with the affairs of Europe and the globe was not a very fortunate one for themselves or for the others. Considering the testimony of the results of German world politics and world conception, they should be justified in admitting that something like a retirement from world history—similar to the one chosen by Switzerland, in the beginning of the 16th century, in all

THE ONLY WAY

freedom and dignity, and not to her detriment—would be for them, too, a good and suitable way out. This would mean that, for the time being, they are not called upon to analyze and to criticize the past of others, and that they must not be concerned with the future of others; that there is only one matter of importance for them, which is that, considering the heap of cinders at the outcome and end of their contribution to world history, to date, their actions should be concentrated only on the small territory left to them. It should dawn on them that no one anywhere expects them to act as the heart, the conscience or the brain of Europe; that is, that they are completely relieved of the obligation to accuse the rest of the world, to give advice and to set up rules—no matter how many such wondrous ideas might pile up in their creative minds! The only thing they are now supposed to do is to turn to the problem of reconstructing German life—unfortunately under conditions created by the German behaviour to date—as well as to the best means of paying for the damage, alas, unquestionably caused by them in the world. From this point of view, a German cure would consist in the admission of the fact that in the near future their opinion will not be required in the wider historical framework. Other peoples, for instance, we

Swiss, do not have any say either, and do not consider this a disgrace or a catastrophe. The question the Germans have to ask themselves is whether they recognize and accept their elimination from world history and their death as a world ruler and a great power and whether this admission will cure them.

The second and third questions concern their internal disagreements. The second points towards the past. It can be nothing else than the question whether the responsibility for all that which happened is to play a major part, for a long time, in the life of the German people. All depends, however, on how this question is worded. Namely, the answer should not lead to a split between Germans and Germans; that is, between the "innocent" and the "guilty," the "honest" and "dishonest"—whenever possible even between Germans from the south and the north—so that, in the end, the Germans should also fight against each other and make life even more unbearable than it already is. The atonement of the German past should not cause the outburst of passions and hatred, however justified. There is no doubt: the "war criminals" will be made to answer for their crimes. It would be only fair that the Germans, who could obviously not rid themselves of these people for the last twelve years, should not try it now and should leave it to the foreign armies and weapons who finally liberated them. It would be wise to leave the difficult task of judging these people to the foreigners and to avoid further bloodshed. Neither is there any doubt: fundamental changes in the political, social and economic structure of the German people will be inevitable and will proceed effectively and irresistibly. And it is to be hoped that especially the Christian churches will not shun this responsibility. But these changes must, from the beginning, avoid taking the form of struggle between groups and classes. Unfortunately, the pernicious habit of thinking collectively is a German characteristic too, which should be eliminated once and for all by taking advantage of the common tribulation. This is not the time to search for all sorts of scape-goats —officers, Prussian Junkers, landowners, great industrialists, etc.—There are, of course, more or less "guilty" groups. Of course, there are conceptions and systems which, considering what happened, should not only be fought, but uprooted; there are also individuals who should vanish from the face of the earth, in the interest of the majority. But the only pertinent and constructive question concerns the guilt in which all groups were involved—the communists as well as the Christian church. There is one point in the question of guilt where all anger against one another is senseless, where all Germans belong together, and they should strive to find this point, and they should openly or silently agree on it; I mean: in a word, all Germans failed to a certain extent—not only some of them, not only this one or that one, because they allowed things to go as far as they have gone.

Now, each group, class, party and faction of the German people should ask: By what error did—I and mine,—I and those who share my opinions contribute to the catastrophe that all of us helped to bring upon ourselves and because of which all of us now suffer? How did we, and not the others, we, with our profoundness or shallowness, our stubbornness or carelessness make possible the miscalculation which lasted from 1933 to 1945? If everyone would dedicate himself to this question, then the Germans of all groups would meet and understand each other. And that should now be achieved.

The third question concerns the future: the positive task of the internal and external reconstruction, which Germany now so urgently needs. From this point of view, to be cured or to be less ill would mean: to cooperate under any circumstances and at any price. What will be the main

THE ONLY WAY

problem of Germany tomorrow, day after tomorrow and for many years to come? Not the filling of the prescription that various individuals at home or abroad might consider best for the common good; not the carrying out of programs already advocated 15 or 50 years ago by different parties, programs which have never been laid before the people but for which the hour now seems to have come! Not in contributing to the victory of some principle—economic, cultural, denominational—which was repudiated in various quarters long ago or at the last moment. To put it plainly, the main question is: how to live under these pitiful conditions, and not only to live but to cooperate. So far, when the Germans were not busy giving and obeying orders, they devised prescriptions, programs and principles in the hope and intention of seizing power one day—the power they all craved! This sort of thing at the moment when the problem of reconstruction becomes tangible should stop instead of developing. There is considerable danger of miracle-mongers popping up at every street corner, old acquaintances and new additions and each of them with his own *Weltanschauung* combined with the suitable social and individual reforms, striving to carry off the palm. Poor German people, if the old party system—we still shudder at the thought of the 23—or were there 37 parties?—in the last German Reichstag—should rise again! This does not have to happen. It is also possible that the small but difficult everyday political questions confronting the Germans everywhere should appear so serious that for the time being they will be compelled to forget with denying their different dogmas, their individual desires and aims, and that they will have to turn to the task at hand without any mental reservation or delay, in order to attain the nearest and most urgent goals, synchronizing them, as much as possible, with the actions of their fellow countrymen. What a blessing if this could almost automatically happen! From this point of view, to be cured, for the Germans, would mean to deal with the everyday political problems as they arise—somewhat as the British and the Swiss do—to discuss the problems together, not to indulge in a clash of ideologies, and throw at each other—conservative, socialist, nationalistic, internationalistic, Christian, atheistic ideas, with the malicious and wicked intention "of seizing power." It would mean to listen to each other at last for the sake of life itself, and to discover and decide together on the best means of achieving a life worth living.

How can the Germans be cured? All the answers

THE ONLY WAY

I gave lead to one and the same point. The German cure depends wholly—and so does the cure of all Europe—on choosing, out of the various human conceptions—and I refer to the Allies as well as to the Germans—the one I would like to mention in my conclusion: Christian Realism. It would, however, be desirable that any study of the answer herein proposed should deal less with this slogan than with its constructive essence.

Letters

LETTERS

I

DEAR PROFESSOR BARTH:

After reading your booklet "The Germans and Ourselves," I decided to write to you. . . . May I hope that you will extend to me the indulgence you requested for the Germans.

No one can deny that establishing relationship with Germany anew constitutes a problem for Switzerland, as well as for all the other countries and that the friendship you advocate appears to be its best solution. This friendship, however, has different aspects, according to the individual frame of mind, being achieved in an easy or arduous way. And I notice throughout your booklet, though the emphasis be on lack of prejudice, the fundamental conception of "Friendship in spite of." This is what I mean to discuss. You invite the Swiss to be friendly with the Germans, assuming, however, the collective guilt of the German people.

To what extent does collective guilt exist? It obviously exists when a majority of united and conscious people take the road to crime. The gang of criminals bears a collective guilt, because each and every one of its members is involved in the crime. But is it possible at all that a whole people, or almost a whole people, be held responsible for a crime, because all its citizens, with few exceptions, contributed to it? I believe that European history does not offer such an example and that not even that which happened during the last 12 years in and because of Germany constitutes such an example. Only in time of war or of war propaganda do peoples manifest different moral standards. In reality, each people has its minority of criminals which indulges in crime in spite of the existence of a constitutional state and law enforcing authority. And each nation has a second and larger minority of potential criminals held in line by laws, but who can readily become criminals whenever the constitutional state breaks down or is replaced by an unconstitutional state, encouraging and rewarding crime, instead of prosecuting and punishing it. When this second and larger minority of criminals comes to the surface because of the breakdown of the constitutional state, it creates the impression of a slackening in morals in this particular nation, as compared with other nations, although it just displays something which exists everywhere but remains hidden. In addition to those two minorities, which constitute but a small percentage, each nation has a powerful majority of "law-abiding citizens," who would not take an active part in crime, whether there be a constitutional state or not. But this powerful majority is definitely not inclined to oppose an active resistance to the outburst of the criminal instincts of the second minority if, because of the above mentioned state of lawlessness, such a resistance would greatly endanger their life and belongings. I will go even farther and state that, within this powerful majority of "law-abiding citizens," there is but a trifling minority of true heroes, fighting injustice at the risk of their very lives. I believe that this sociological classification of crime and reaction against crime has manifested itself with surprising regularity in all nations, in times of political crisis, developing according to the seriousness of the situation. That which is considered a difference in moral standards is always superficial, when nations are concerned, and is in reality a difference in the fundamental, especially in the constitutional premises.

I hope that you will not consider this as a "dangerous twist" in the apology, and the less so, since I am prepared to give you a trivial but concrete example. When the United States, towards the end of the first world war, introduced prohibition, it failed to provide the means necessary to enforce this law. As a result of this very limited breakdown of the constitutional state, the following years witnessed an unthinkable crime wave, which started with bootlegging and extended to other criminals fields, leading to organized blackmail and kidnapping. At the same time, a real and deadly war broke out between the competing gangs. The statistics of criminology reached unbelievable heights, and little by little, the United States appeared as a country of criminals.

This however was an internal problem of the United States. The world at large began to discuss very much the moral weakness of the United States, although the gangsters of Chicago were not considered as representing the true American spirit. In reality, this does not constitute an indictment against the morals of the American people, but merely shows how the perfectly normal sociological division into moral and immoral can produce the most unexpected phenomena.

The leading clique of the Third Reich was branded as gangster from the very beginning. But little did people understand how true this comparison really was. There is only a difference in

THE ONLY WAY

size. The outside world as well as the state itself became the hunting ground of the gangsters. But the moral evaluation of the Germans does not depend on differences, but rather on the similarities. I believe we should once and for all give up the habit of deciding on the moral standards of nations, believing all which war propaganda so willingly spread. All European nations are morally neutral, colorless and undecided. From a collective point of view, none of them can be praised or condemned. There are national differences based on aptitudes and talents, taste and tradition, which condition the professional abilities, but certainly not morals.

There is no such thing as collective guilt of the German people for National Socialism, and therefore there should be no question of collective punishment, notwithstanding the fact that no earthly power is qualified to act as judge. There is no guilt of all the German people, because there never was and never will be collective guilt involving a whole nation. Somehow, many people seem to have today the yearning of attributing the gigantic events that came to pass to causes as gigantic. This leads to the strange puzzle woven around the German nature and history. The limited guilt that exists, obviously does not satisfy the people's desire for

THE ONLY WAY

determining the cause. They blow it up in space, so that it covers the whole country; and in time, until it covers history. In this respect, your attitude is not isolated, but I deplore your endorsing such a trend, for I expected something else from you, something less simplified, less generalized, less embittered, in a word, more friendly. What Germany now needs is friendship based on a correct diagnosis, not friendship in spite of a false diagnosis. It is not so important today to swallow the actual collective wrath in a Christian and courageous way when meeting a German, but to let light pierce and dispel the foggy image of the collective wrath before meeting him. Otherwise, I fear the meeting will be sterile. One should not try to forget the past, in order to find a new approach in the relationship with Germans in a "Pro" without consideration for the quality of the object, while the abandoned past was labelled plainly "Anti," because it considered the quality of the object. The attitude towards the German people must be cleared of the "ira et studium" before the meeting, and also of the swallowed "ira et studium."

And referring to that which has been said above about the sociological division, the following must now be emphasized: heroism is a great virtue, but lack of heroism is not a crime. I do not mean the

THE ONLY WAY

cheap version of heroism, concerned only with "glory and honor" or with soldierly recklessness, but the other one, the only one which interests us here, the one based only on one's conscience, the heroism which is ready to accept even "shameful death." Such heroes are always and everywhere the exception rather than the rule. One has the right to be surprised when meeting them, and not if one does not meet them. Some of the things you said seem to imply that only those who resisted during the last twelve years should be accepted, and the others should be declared guilty. But that which deserves the name "resistance," in a totalitarian state demands this last and highest form of heroism which is bound to remain an exception. When a situation arises which can only be overcome if a whole people consists of heroes, each of them resisting individually, such a situation cannot be overcome. The last twenty years should have taught us that a totalitarian state can hardly be overthrown from within—and if then, not by the people—, but fundamentally only from the outside. The true heroic resistance of the individual was found to be useless, as well as fatal. Are you then surprised that it was not widespread? It is known that quite a number of people suffered in concentration camps and stood before the people's court. But not even a majority of those can be considered as real martyrs. A careless word, even though not followed by action, or a mere denunciation, that is all that was needed. As far as I know, Martin Niemoeller himself has denied the charges, brought against him, not from the point of view of legality, but of content. He is supposed to have stated that he did not mean to attack the national socialist state as such. Martyrdom? There was much suffering, but little resistance.

The percentage of heroes is much smaller than that of criminals. There are no statistics so far, and there will probably never be any, but I believe that the impression most men have about the rate of political and police crimes in Germany should be greatly revised. I believe that an estimate giving the figure of those who participated in the inhuman treatment of people in and outside of Germany as two hundred thousand would be exaggerated. That would mean one criminal for every four hundred Germans, or an inhuman being for every four hundred human beings. In addition, there are those second-class criminals who were not involved in anything of the sort, but who acquired wealth by means considered criminal in a constitutional state. Let us put into this category two hundred thousand more Germans, and this is

THE ONLY WAY

probably much too high a figure, since a Robber state gives a free hand in robbery to the upper crust only. And let us hope there were fifty thousand heroes. Then, we are still left with 99% of the Germans who are not guilty of actually committing crimes, without being worthy of the name of heroes.

Now, can 200,000 real, inhuman criminals be considered an exceptionally high number? For the sake of human optimism, it would be desirable. But, in the interest of truth, it has to be denied. For it has been unfortunately proven that, in each and every European country where the same problem arose, the very same type of evil power-seekers and evil forces keeping them in power emerged from the underworld, where they seem to be available in the desired number. Such were the Quislings and the Degrelles, Musserts, Lavals and Pawelitschs; such are the hords of Rexists, and the French Legions and the "Germanic" SS of the Baltic states and so many others. They appeared as soon as they had a chance and their inhuman behavior is in no way attenuated by the fact that they acted on a smaller scene and a less interested public. And they topped the list of their crimes by becoming traitors to their own countries. I believe that after all these experiences, no country on earth could claim in all sincerity that one out of every four hundred of its citizens would not prove himself to be such an inhuman being if given a chance, and ready to serve an inhuman system to the end. That which you insist in calling the "German actions" and because of which all Germany becomes a puzzle to be morally distrusted, are the actions of a trifling minority and as unrepresentative of the German people as the Schalburg-Corps is of the Danish.

But, you and many others will undoubtedly object: It might be true, that the German people did not have the opportunity of overthrowing the totalitarian state once it was firmly established and that since 1933 the whole structure consisted of a few criminals, of very few heroes and an endless chain of innocent people. There is, however, a difference in the case of Norway, France, etc., as compared with Germany: namely that the German people helped National Socialism to come to power, they even called them to power. With this objection which requires a detailed answer, January 30, 1933 becomes the decisive day of German history, the day on which depends the question of guilt or innocence of the German people. If this day be the key to the German guilt, then we may decide whether the previous events of German or Prussian history led to this January 30. I for one, strongly

THE ONLY WAY

deny this. I wish to end this letter without stating my reasons and without indulging again in gangster examples. I have taken up too much of your valuable time already. But before taking leave, I would like to know if you find this correspondence useful and if you wish to make your contribution to it.

Very respectfully yours

....

DEAR SIR:

Please accept my thanks for having gone into the trouble of writing me at such length. I read your very interesting letter with great attention and I wish to answer you at once.

The thesis you presented to me is very cleverly built up and quite impressive. But I am unable to agree with it. I consider it merely as a form of brain acrobatics, meant to provide a way to escape reality. It could not possibly be of any real help to the German people. I will now proceed to state my objections point by point.

Let us suppose that you are right. In this case, we should have called to the Germans the day after their defeat: "Something awful has happened for which we hold you all responsible. However, this would be unjust. After all, during all this

THE ONLY WAY

time, 99% of you were perhaps no heroes, but neither were you criminals. You were "law-abiding" citizens, and, as such, not guilty of any crime. You acted exactly as 99% of any other nation would have done under similar circumstances. The ½% German criminals may be hanged, the ½% German heroes may be praised, with some reservation. Anyhow, you, the 99%, are acquitted." According to your thesis, the same speech could and even should have been made to the German people, the very day of the Anglo-French declaration of war, in 1939, or even on July 1, 1934, or on January 31, 1933, and so on. If you were right, this same speech should be made to you, today, on the eve of your defeat, when you are still ganging up with Hitler. The 99% righteous ones held and still hold the same advantageous position. This prompts me to ask two questions:

1. Do you really think that the relationship between the Germans and their present adversaries would be improved if they were confronted with the latter, armed with those arguments? When and where did something else than "caught together, hanged together," or in its more classical form *Quidquid delirant reges, plectuntur Achivi* apply to the lives of nations? Will not I, as a Swiss, be held responsible for all eternity and to a certain

THE ONLY WAY

extent suffer with the rest for whatever harm the Confederate Government has caused by its way of expressing the Swiss opinion before the world during those last years, although I, as a law-abiding citizen, only stood by and even occasionally protested. The 99% law-abiding Germans took, each and all, the wrong train, after being warned in vain. And this train brought them today to the point where they again, each and all, must get off together. They were for once *ibi* and not *alibi*.

2. Do you think that it would be good for the Germans to build the future with the conviction of being innocent, thanks to your thesis? Would that not mean that the 99% irresponsible citizens will start waiting again—and this time with reason —for somebody to appear from somewhere—perhaps out of the ½% newly born heroes to lead them, or perhaps out of the ½% newly born criminals—and to decide by himself the question of future German guilt or innocence, while the 99% law-abiding citizens will, as usual, merely stand by and watch, which means be accomplices to whatever happens, and still be considered innocent? How else could these 99% be helped if they do not decide to step forward this very day and partake in the responsibility for the future instead of trying to shove it on someone else? And

why would they do that if they do not admit they were guilty yesterday of leading politically irresponsible lives? I cannot help but think that anyone who would comfort the Germans by advocating their innocence, as you now do, Dear Sir, would be their worst enemy. Whoever wishes them well cannot and should not let them get away with it so easily.

I would now like to try to answer the more important details of your letter.

1. I am not so much concerned with guilt in itself, or collective guilt. I do not mention them in my lectures. I am very much in favor of the Germans, and I mean all the Germans, admitting their responsibility for all that which happened since 1933. And by this I do not mean so much, the crimes committed as the road that lead and had to lead to those crimes. Comparatively few Germans must have taken part in the crimes themselves. But they all took the road leading to these crimes, either in the form of actions or negligence, of direct or indirect participation, of explicit or tacit consent, of unequivocal, active or "pro forma" party membership, of political indifference or in the form of all kinds of political errors and miscalculations. How else could the "small minority of criminals" triumph and National Socialism make world his-

THE ONLY WAY

tory. To achieve this, all Germans had to participate, including your 99% righteous people, be it even in the most different ways. Nobody intends to put the German people as a whole, with all its members, on the list of war criminals. How is it possible that any German over 21 should not admit that he belongs, in one way or another, to those who succeeded in bringing the German people to the point where the whole world had to unite to fight the threat so gigantic because of the masses it represented—how does your percentage fit into this?

2. The American parallel you develop, fails to prove your point because of the following reasons: However inefficient the measures taken by the American government and the 99% law-abiding citizens against the gangsters, two things did not happen: (a) the gangsters did not move in the White House, with or without the consent of the people and the American State as such did not become a gangster-state, whose president, for instance, would have dared engineer a June 30, 1934. (b) The United States, even had it been led with or without its consent by gangsters, did not become a menace for other nations and did not provoke a war against itself. The fact that the German state itself became—first by its domestic, then

by its foreign policy—the hunting ground, even the instrument of gangsters, constitutes, in my opinion, a fundamental difference. I cannot believe that, considering all this, you wish to uphold your statement that, under the same, somewhat fantastic circumstances, the same thing could and would happen in the United States or other countries. Maybe. But only in Germany, in Germany alone did it really happen.

3. Neither can I accept your comparison between the German gangsters and the foreign Quislings, etc., those disciples of the German school! You must know that, for instance, the Danish Schalburg-Corps was not accepted with indifference, but rejected by the Danish people in the most evident way. The same thing happened to the followers of Mussert, in Holland, the Rexists, in Belgium and the collaborationists in France, and this, mostly, not only after liberation, but very firmly even under German occupation. Your comparison would be acceptable if German public opinion would have expressed itself in the same way, be it only once, against the traitors of the German state. Instead of which, the SS and SA found the road absolutely free. I do not understand how a thing which has been tolerated, as National-Socialism has been by the German people, in its

days of glory, can be now shaken off as if it never existed. It seems to me that this is unfair—even to the gangsters.

4. If I were asked: Who was responsible for what happened in Germany, the ½% gangsters or the 99% law-abiding citizens, I would answer without hesitation: The latter, the "law-abiding citizens." They had recognized and approved the constitutional state, at least to a certain extent, a thing Hitler never did. They were morally and legally its supporters and trustees. And they were the ones who betrayed it. And by "they" I mean, for example, all German professors and other members of the university faculties, mainly German nationalists, but also liberals and democrats, whose capitulation and conversion I had the opportunity to witness with my own eyes in 1933. They and the German judges, civil servants, ministers, authors, artists, etc., who chose to go the way of all flesh by the thousands fit obviously and even very well, into your classification, that is, as belonging to the group of the 99% righteous ones. And should these very people be given an alibi, and acquitted, or given the privilege of acquitting themselves, just because they were not present in person at Oradour, or perhaps never even heard of Oradour? Should these wretched

THE ONLY WAY

German intellectuals with their philosophy of versatility of principles be allowed to watch happily the "criminals" being hanged and to go on quietly vegetating in their irresponsible attitude towards the state, until the next cataclysm occurs? How should things ever change in this poor Germany, if the righteous do not admit that they should retrace their steps and prove by their actions that they disavow their past conduct?

5. The Frederick-Bismarck-Hindenburg-Hitler policy was not discovered and applied outside of Germany, but in Germany itself and mostly by the same 99% efficient German nationals and also by the recognized representatives and interpreters of the Frederick-Bismarck-Wilhelm tradition. Only in Germany did qualified historians eloquently praise, or at least tacitly accept this tradition.

6. I do not agree with your statement that the German nation would have had to consist only of heroes, in order to avoid the National Socialist catastrophe. It would have had to consist merely of politically reasonable citizens ready to act, or of citizens quietly remaining in their places. Resistance would have come by itself in each civil servant who would have refused to carry out unconstitutional and crazy regulations; in each professor and teacher who would have stood by the

scientific truth, as it was previously known to him; in each minister who would have continued to preach the uncorrupted teaching of the Gospel; in each officer who would have clung to what he considered his honor in the past; in each common man who would have insisted on his constitutional rights. Heroism? No, healthy conception of citizenship. Maturity instead of hopeless tutelage. Dear Sir, let me remind you that I myself lived through these events for several years. I saw that the totalitarian state did not strike the Germans suddenly like irresistible lightning, but that it started long before the so called seizing of power. I saw how, while the totalitarian state was making its claws felt little by little, thus getting the upper hand, all, or almost all, gave up their legal ground inch by inch; how ordinary people became heroes easily liquidated one by one, until the inches became yards and miles and everything was converted into a pliable mass, to the point where the German people became the most hated and the most bitterly fought enemy of all other nations. What did they need? The very thing I call healthy conception of citizenship and maturity. And because the German people should reach a healthy conception of citizenship and maturity, the German people should not be comforted by the thought that it is impossible for a whole nation to be a nation of heroes. As if it were necessary to be a hero in order not to be a dish-rag. The British are certainly far from being a nation of heroes. Neither are they a nation of dish-rags. *Tertium datur.* And it is about time that the Germans should find a third way too.

The terms of my theory, as expressed in the 6 points given above make it clear that the essence of my opposition to your thesis can be expressed in this one question: Who other than the German people allowed national socialism to seize power, even called it to power? I wonder if, after my answer, you still feel like giving me a lecture on the date of January 30, 1933. You can already see, that which I do not want to express here a priori, that the German people should become aware of its responsibility in the lack of responsibility shown on January 30, 1933, and do away with a system to which it fell victim after the 30 years war or since the Peasants' war and the end of the constitutional state.

Before finishing my letter, I want to confirm the fact that my speech was truly concerned with "friendship in spite of." This point struck many other Germans. I do not even intend to admit that this is the weak point of my lecture. You must not forget that this speech was not addressed to the Germans, but to the Swiss. Do not underestimate the fact that I clung to the teaching of the Gospel: *justificatio impii*. Without taking the quality of the object into consideration. I could say more than I already said. I may still say it some other time. But this more will certainly not consist in an excuse for the Germans, in the sense advocated by them, nor in a retroactive accusation of Bismarck and Frederick.

Very sincerely yours

KARL BARTH.

II

Dear Professor Barth:

A few days ago, I had the opportunity of reading your pamphlet, "The Germans and Ourselves." As a German, I was so deeply impressed that I feel the urge of writing to you. I do not intend to bother you with lengthy developments on each point of your pamphlet—with which I agree without reservations—but to tell you how deeply moved I was, as a human being and as a Christian, in feeling again a manifestation of warm and friendly understanding. Your approach to the German problem seems to me the only and last possibility of tackling the question of the German future in a constructive way, that is, to try with human warmth, with—let us dare name it—Christian love, to arouse like with like, to make germinate the seeds, which, in spite of everything, must still slumber in the devastated land. One must try to bring the other Germany, the Germany which is master of its own destiny and which is only spiritually mature, on this earth, at last.

THE ONLY WAY

You are absolutely right when you suppose that a certain percentage of the German people were body and soul against the awesome Nazi regime from the very beginning. Those who, like myself, come from a family which suffered greatly because of its convictions, know what opposition could achieve during those 12 years, and what it could not: From a practical point of view, it was absolutely useless. The German bourgeoisie dug, however, its own grave by its exaggerated passivity. But who could accuse the lamb for being unable to bite the wolf? The more constructive, cooler heads among us, Southern Germans, were precisely the ones that do not make for good rebels and National Socialism knew admirably well how to appear under hundreds of enticing disguises, and offering each decent German the aspect which appealed to him, thus throwing dust into people's eyes so that they could not see what evil forces were de facto masters of the German fatherland. This is meant as an explanation, not as an excuse. The question: "what is the position of the German citizen today?" can only be answered, according to my own experience, by saying: "None, whatsoever, no matter which layer of the population we consider." He is frightfully broken morally and—whether laborer or president of a corporation—he

THE ONLY WAY

gave up thinking in depth, as well as in intensity; some drew a dividing line between practical and moral life and abandoned all hope of reconciling them. I would like to mention at this point that although the brute and astutely applied Nazi power has been criticized and branded in all its manifestations, in foreign countries, and especially by neutrals, nobody seems to have come to the obvious conclusion that the first victims of this tightly woven net were to be found in Germany itself.

I sometimes wonder if a firm opposition of all true, reasonable Germans would have achieved more than an honorable finale, for death at the hand of Nazi hangmen would have been as certain as it later was on the battlefield or will be in the coming period of starvation. Human beings will survive in Germany only as an integral part of the mass, as Ortega y Gasset so accurately said. But—and in this respect my perspective is much more pessimistic than yours, dear Professor Barth—does the world outside Germany really strive for the attainment of a higher human and moral level? Are the symptoms of a similar collective craze not unmistakably apparent among the Allies? A permanent vengeance against the German—alias Nazi—evil doings? Inhumanity for inhumanity and so on? Isn't it about time to stop the bloodthirsty fury of

THE ONLY WAY

neverending revenge? Someone has to take the first step. And I do not mean so much in the name of human or Christian dignity and greatness, but purely for practical and rational reasons. Instead of which, the tendencies to such a conduct are hindered by the allied prohibition of fraternization with the civilian population of Germany.

Your opinion on the degeneration and deprivation of the Germans in the evil tradition of a Frederick the Great, Bismarck and Hitler, plus their numerous epigons found a response in my soul, but I often am overcome by the nightmare—may I be wrong—that this cancer may be only the early and special outbreak of a more general, a world disease, for the cure of which the western allies now hold a last, a tempting and great possibility, and especially, among the allies, those who sing: "Onward Christian Soldiers!" But is not the "Christian" on their lips only sounding brass and a tinkling cymbal? Can one build great hopes on those nations? The Nazis murdered hundreds of thousands of innocent Jews, Poles, French, Dutch, Russians—and even Germans—the latter, in turn, murdered a few really guilty ones, many doubtful guilty ones and masses of innocent people. Will it go on like this for ever? We should be just. Murder remains murder, crime remains crime.

THE ONLY WAY

Unless I am very much mistaken, an attempt will be made to paralyze, or even to wipe out the German people. An attempt will be made to render a new start impossible, be it purely spiritual or even Christian. Everything will be done in order to hinder the ability of spiritual regeneration, so characteristic of the Germans. You will be able to witness this tragedy from the other side of the Swiss border, if a faint rumor of the gigantic tragedy can leak out and cross the border. At close range, however, the chaos will choke up any trace of aesthetic or moral activity. The saying: "Operation successful, patient dead," will become a terrible reality. It is natural, that I, although an enemy of the Nazis, should oppose and fight this, as any German would. Will the destruction of a people which created men like Heine, Goethe, Beethoven, Eichendorff, Schubert, and more recently a Th. Mann and Hermann Hesse not constitute a dangerous precedent? I am afraid that as a reversal of the biblical parable, the beam from the German eye will be removed with great ado, in order to avoid worrying about the thousands and thousands of motes which cover all humanity. It is so pleasant to be able to avoid expurgation of oneself by flogging a suitable scapegoat.

I know from my own experience how great is

THE ONLY WAY

the desire of many Germans to establish human contacts again, even with their former enemies. What was the use of all the suffering, of the other nations as well as ours, if a new light should not shine over humanity, in as much as it conserves even a remote and blurred tie with the blood shed on Golgotha, if "Humanitas," as defined by Nicholas of Cusa, the reflection represented in the finite the infinite man-God, Jesus Christ should not spread its wings anew over the world.

May all at last realize that the third world war cannot be avoided by muzzling German science, by letting German children starve and by offering German babies, crying for want of food, the example of Auschwitz. People should be made to understand that German Hitlerism cannot be uprooted in the midst of world-Hitlerism, but only by trying to plant in all nations a spirit in which such monstrosities cannot survive.

May I be forgiven for writing you at such length.
With kindest regards,
     Yours truly,

DEAR SIR:
I wish to thank you for your letter. It moved me deeply, because it brought further proof of the difficult situation which faces Germany today. It

brought me also joy and hope, proving that a German can have such a full understanding of the situation. That is why I cannot leave your argumentation unanswered. We agree on so many and such important points. Can you and will you advance further on my side?

May I first express a few thoughts on the Christian background of your letter. Not true: "As Christians, we cannot indulge in pessimistic prospects." Of course, neither in optimistic ones; perhaps in no prospects at all, but in a bare and decided and essential comforting view and conception of human things in their hard but not God forsaken reality. We Christians must come today from the spheres where everything is run in a smooth and orderly way, without our contributing anything. That is what Jesus Christ's resurrection means for us. That is why we and all humans, no matter how dark things look, cannot and must not give up. That is why we must keep our composure even when faced with the greatest calamities this century ever saw. This is what I pleaded for in Switzerland, and with my French friends, in 1940 when Hitler's star was at its Zenith. This is what I want to plead for with the Germans today. I am now thinking of Albrecht Dürer's "Knight between Death and Devil." Much ado has been made in

THE ONLY WAY

Bismarck's, Wilhelm's and Hitler's Germany as to the symbolical meaning of this painting. It is time for the Germans to understand now its original meaning, for this painting was inspired by passages Eph. 6, 10–17 of the New Testament. Read them. Then this picture can constitute a lesson for the Germany of today. These words should be proclaimed by the sound of trumpets throughout the German cities which lay in ruins.

But this very point makes me think that Germany needs now more than an attempt to "bring the other Germany, the Germany which is master of its own destiny and which is only spiritually mature, on this earth again." The question is not, as you later seem to imply, the unveiling of the values and the recognition of Christ's resurrection, which existed in the "Spiritual inner sanctum" of German idealists and to take this hidden treasure out of study-rooms and make it part of the everyday life of the German people. According to my knowledge of German affairs, the problem is largely to bring the so called "spiritually mature" Germany to a new way of thinking and a new conception of life. Dear German Idealists of all varieties, beware! Who else but those very people you call "bourgeoisie" and "constructive minds" dug not only their own, but the whole nation's grave? Were they not the ones who forgot to assume responsibility for the German nation, by drawing a line between their moral and their political lives and by then linking them together. This attitude enabled the idealists to keep in their hearts a community of spirit with all the great minds of humanity, living it with an intensity seldom found outside of Germany; but it also permitted and even compelled them to adore other Gods in their public lives, in a passive, but unfortunately also quite active way, in a silent, but sometimes rather eloquent manner. The German problem does not lie in Bismarck and Hitler, but in the adjustment of the German intellect to Bismarck and Hitler; in the weakness and versatility which enabled and even compelled the German spirit, up to now, to answer, as a spirit to the anti-spiritual, "no" in private, "yes" in public; in their characteristic ability to consciously live in two conflicting spheres. I know from many sources that, this time, as the disaster was threatening—and the more it became imminent—these circles regretted and repented for having started it all; that, in individual cases, they tried to help Jews and prisoners of war, and were even secretly pleased with the Allied advance. How relieved I was at the news that German hands, at last, had actively contributed to the German liberation, when the Allies crossed the Rhine around Remagen! How happy would I be, as a former professor of the University of Bonn if it were true that the success was due in part to the efficient participation of a group of students of Bonn. But you must understand, as I do, that such isolated and belated proofs of conversion can not compensate for the leadership that the German spirit owed but failed to give the German people in the years 1860 to 1890 and then later at the ascension, and during the rule of the Hitlerite usurpation and which it still owes the German people. In 1933, I saw the masses of those same professors and students of Bonn busy with quite different things. Should then that which must leave the study room and come out into the open be nothing more than a new aspect of the much too dialectical German spirit, should this only be another disguise of that "lamb" which not only cannot bite the wolf, but cannot even resist bleating his approval, then I cannot very well see how anything can be gained by revealing these hidden values. We only hope that something might happen in the spiritual inner sanctum which never happened there before, namely that the German "bourgeoisie," in as far as it still exists, should become at last really "bourgeois," that the German spirit—and above all the German Christian spirit

THE ONLY WAY

—should not seek its expression in art anymore, that it should not, in some false depth, ally himself to the devil, in the name of God. Instead, it should stand up like a man and discover and prove its real depth by becoming openly and honestly politically minded and by assuming responsibilities in the political arena.

There is so much material for thought and action that I wish to offer some corrections concerning your opinions on the world situation as a whole.

You have the tendency to consider all that happens today in the world as a vicious circle: one cruelty, one act of violence against another one, murder against murder. Is it really that simple? It is sad but unfortunately true that the destruction of the national socialist threat had to take the form of a world war against national socialist Germany —no other approach would have succeeded—. It is sadder still, but also true that the extraordinary and treacherous stature of the national socialist threat required extraordinary means of defense and brought upon Germany the total war, invented in and applied by Germany itself. The nation which elected Hitler chose at the same time to wage and to suffer total war. It invited especially the strategy of the western allies; that is, total destruction of the war machine maintained by the

THE ONLY WAY

German people as a whole and sparing as much as possible the lives of their own soldiers; this led them to avoid slaughter which nearly bled them to death in 1916–1918. The fact that this tragedy cost so many German lives is indeed deplorable. I, however—although many British and Americans strongly and loudly disagree with me on this point—do not think that this should be called murder, nor that the use of block-busters should be at all compared with Oradour and Auschwitz. In spite of all the sympathy we have for the German victims, we simply cannot admit that the annihilation of the peasants of Oradour and of the Jews, in Auschwitz, falls into the same category with the bombardment of the German industry and communication centers in the interest of winning the war by trying to break the impetus of attack and resistance in a nation mobilized for total war. What Hitler planned for the German nation and, with the help of the German nation, could not be allowed to become reality for the outside world, under any circumstances. It shall not become reality. An attempt unparalleled against the people of the world—and against the German people—has been stemmed. War was the price that had to be paid. It stands to reason that Germany had to be the one hardest hit. I think, however, that

THE ONLY WAY

decent and fair Germans should not seize this opportunity and throw the treacherous attempt and the war waged against it in the same pot.

I also wish to warn you against the assumption that, after their victory, the Allies intend to take a horrible revenge on Germany. It cannot be denied that the V-bomb caused recently, even in England, all kinds of outbursts of hatred and revenge. I also deem it possible that in the East and, perhaps, even in the West—at least in French territory—violent acts of revenge will and did occur, not to mention the army of 12 million liberated slave workers. You are, however, most certainly mistaken if you think that the official attitude of America and England or even Stalin will have anything to do with "revenge and retaliation." No serious and responsible man thinks of the annihilation of the German people or the muzzling of German science. Some previous representatives of German science might possibly be invited to dedicate the rest of their lives to private studies, but, even from your point of view, this could not be considered as a major disaster. And if, God forbid, next winter should bring starvation to Germany—after, thanks to the Germans, the same thing happened to the Norwegians, Dutch, Poles, Greeks and many others —it will be due entirely—unless German actions

THE ONLY WAY

and enterprises make further reprisals necessary—to the lack of Allied shipping facilities and not at all in order to make German babies pay for Auschwitz. Things are bad enough as they are. Let us not be unnecessarily pessimistic. What the Allies must obviously have in view for Germany is the establishment of an order which would prevent it from waging a third world war and its participation in the reconstruction of devastated territories, even beyond its borders. Nothing very serious has as yet happened, and it would therefore be wise for us all to reserve our judgment, and it would be particularly desirable for the Germans to do so. You see, dear sir, your trend of thought is not appropriate and inadvisable because, at its best, it is based on the assumption that we live in the dark, where all cats are grey. There is one thing I am afraid of and to which I wish to draw the attention of the Germans, namely the waste of time and energy, which would not change their situation in the least, but on account of which they might miss the opportunity of changing their way of life, which has been proven to be a failure and of leaving with a decided step the path which brought the hatred and wrath of the whole world upon them. The Germans should not try to dodge this *unum necessarium*. I dislike those untimely ac-

THE ONLY WAY

cusations brought by the Germans against the Allies especially because it would be so much better and more courageous for the Germans to dedicate all their efforts, now and for a long time to come, exclusively to the questions they have to ask themselves.

I would like to make a third point on the same subject. You are afraid that the moral level of humanity will not rise even after this war, and that on the contrary, the German collective craze might spread to the Allied camp and become the source of new catastrophes. Let us examine what the correct meaning of this is. Not even in Sunday schools, in America, where almost anything is possible, does one teach that Hitler's downfall would be followed by one thousand years of peace and justice on earth. Man will always be man, and even more so after such troubled times, that he is, as the Reformed Church acknowledges, "naturally inclined" to hate his "God and his neighbor." There is no prophecy about human progress. It is even possible that, due to changed conditions, we become worse and worse. I believe nevertheless that we should not speculate on this situation—neither on a rise nor on a fall—but that we should remain on the point of the line—leading upwards or downwards—on which we happen to be, armed with the tendency

THE ONLY WAY

befitting the sons of Adam, of eliminating any disorder which might occur somewhere and of reestablishing the state of things that used to prevail. What do we know about the possible collective moral level in the future? And why should we try to know? Is it not enough that each day—and this is well known to each of us—has its share of trouble. The trouble of the last 12 years was the German national socialism. Our task, and most of all, the German task, consists in uprooting it, its causes and consequences, and once this done, to begin anew. The next 12 years might bring us a new, and perhaps greater calamity. How can we know what may already be brewing in America or in Russia? But, we can be assured of three things: 1. That this new calamity did not start yet. 2. That, should it come, it will be different, and in no way a repetition of that of yesterday and of today, of the national socialist calamity. 3. That the victors and not the Germans will be responsible for it this time. Is it just and is it wise to start examining the future through field-glasses—before even thanking God for the end of Nazism, before even tackling the task which incumbers the Germans—worrying about the danger that might threaten from America, Russia or any other place, perhaps thus overlooking the duty to be performed

THE ONLY WAY

today and today only? I do not consider this melancholy staring into the future and possibly into another melancholy as advisable. And I would not like my friends, the Germans, to be plunged again into this sterile melancholy which has probably already played a harmful part in the preceeding events. "As we speak, oh my God, time flies by." The German speeches of "collective moral level" accompanied by impressive gestures are but a waste of time and energy as well as an attempt to avoid the issues, instead of striving to improve slightly their own moral standards. All of us, dear sir, even we non-Germans, we, all the peoples and all countries can but do our part, according to our discernment and abilities, wherever we see a little stretch of beaten road, each of us in his circle and according to his profession, for the accomplishment of the gigantic task which lies ahead. In this spirit, I travelled through one half of Switzerland with the speech to which I owe your friendly answer and, although having no illusions as to the effectiveness of my endeavors, I must admit that as a whole, I encountered sympathy and no ill will. A serious effort is bound to engender effort in others.

And now I would like to end my long answer to your long letter with a practical proposition. Do you happen to know that we have in Switzerland

THE ONLY WAY

a "Movement for a Free Germany" supported by Germans of all political parties and shades, aiming at unity and understanding between all Germans now in Switzerland, towards a constructive policy in the post-war fatherland. I am telling you what I told to your compatriots I happened to meet: Instead of sitting under a weeping willow, they should join this movement, make it their own, help to make it strong. Every free German, and judging by the ideas expressed in your letter, I consider you as one of them, should do that. Do not be afraid of meeting a few communists. You will have to live with communists in the future Germany too. Start taking part of your own free will right now! The address is: "Bewegung Freies Deutschland," Postfach Fraumünster, Zürich. Excuse my being so insistent. But as a Swiss I simply cannot stand by and see how many Germans, who do not stop worrying about their fatherland, evade the practical step which would enable them to help right away and on the spot, or postpone it for I do not know when, as if anything could become more urgent than it already has become.

Very sincerely yours,

KARL BARTH.

Part 2

The Germans and Ourselves

I have chosen this theme because I personally am greatly concerned about it. I am searching for the right answer to the question which is contained in it. I shall certainly be able to do no more than indicate the direction in which I am searching. But I cannot forbear pointing out that at least the search for the right answer to this question should be the concern of us all, or certainly of as many as possible.

By the "Germans" of whom I wish to speak I understand the German people of today, which at the end and goal of a long achievement has sold itself, or at least submitted, to National-Socialism, and whose fault and fate it is that it has to stand or fall by this system.

And by "ourselves" I understand us, the Swiss, at the beginning of the year 1945; I also presuppose that we are not only Swiss in all the human and political significance of the term, but also that over and above this we want to be addressed and taken seriously as Christians.

But what is the question here? I should like first

THE ONLY WAY

to recall two facts which were recounted in our newspapers in the last weeks of 1944.

It happened that in Basel, in and with the stream of Alsatian refugees, who received a friendly welcome, there also crossed our frontier a band of fugitive German soldiers. An S.S. officer had tried to prevent their doing this. They had shot him. They were obviously not only war-weary, but also Hitler-weary. But they still wore German uniform. They were then, as wearers of this uniform, abused and insulted and spat upon, in the streets of one of our suburbs, by the Swiss public—and especially, it is said, by women.

And it happened, shortly after, that at a meeting of some very responsible persons who were organizing and administering the well known "Swiss Fund" for the relief of distress abroad, one member felt obliged to warn the meeting in all seriousness against our including our neighbours in Germany in this help: if they did, it would be all up with the popularity and thus with the success of the proposed appeal for money.

I may surely suppose without further ado that we deplore and disapprove of such incidents—the first more strongly, the second perhaps less strongly. But let each of us now examine himself: we do not oppose these things without a certain under-

THE ONLY WAY

standing of them and perhaps even a slight agreement with them. Which of us in recent years has not experienced the mood in which, given the opportunity and the freedom from certain moral scruples, we would have said and done the very same? That we have at least entertained such thoughts we shall scarcely be able, and perhaps do not even want, to deny. Today a fundamental distrust of the Germans as such, a deep alienation from these neighbours of ours, perhaps even the desire that we should hear and see no more of them, lurks to some extent in us all.

It was not always so. During the war of 1870 in French-speaking Switzerland, and during the war of 1914 in German-speaking Switzerland, it was without any doubt not so. Even at the beginning of the Hitler régime and even at the beginning of this war it was still not so. The Swiss are not easily discomposed, or persuaded to forego their natural leaning towards reserve and impartiality. In themselves they are not really German-haters. Those who knew or thought they knew what was happening or threatening to happen across the frontiers, received from us at first only a very partial hearing. At first we were far more inclined to mistrust the emigrés, the Jews, and then the Allied propaganda, than the Germans, whom we thought we knew to be, with certain reserves, quite different. We showed—just as the English did—a certain mild interest in National-Socialism, and in consequence we were the more reserved towards the German opposition, the Confessional Church and, later, even Hitler's enemies in the war. We had to be slowly taught by bitter experience, which admitted of no dispute—and many, besides, who would be still unconvinced today, needed to be taught by a brilliant series of Russian, English and American victories—before a decisive change was effected. This change has now been effected. What the Germany of our generation has purposed and desired, what it has made of men and done with men has in the last few years become clear in a terrible crescendo even to those who earlier refused to see it.

Correspondingly there has developed a general disillusionment, depression, indignation and resentment with which we really did not wish to regard our neighbours, but to which there is now no alternative. We Swiss must now so regard them, even though we suffered only indirectly, and for the most part merely by our sympathy for what happened to others, as the result of what this German people has planned and done. "I can no longer think of the Germans as men," wrote a French

THE ONLY WAY

writer recently, as he looked back over all he had seen in those years with his own eyes. Today we understand such a remark, even if we do not echo it. It had to end like this. It would certainly not have been fitting if, as was desired of us for so long, Swiss military neutrality had developed into a mental and political neutrality. We were, indeed, not attacked by this Germany; but in truth we were sufficiently threatened. For the sake of our independence, of all that we as Swiss people have to stand for, it was essential for us to be clear about our spiritual opposition to the present-day Germans, and moreover to proclaim it in every form. It was not really a prudent but a dangerous policy, which for a time tried to prevent our doing this.

But now that the lesson has been learnt and the change of mind has become general, the question of "the Germans and ourselves" confronts us in real earnest; the question of what, now that we have reached this stage, must really be the relation between them and ourselves; the question of what is the first *new* word that must follow the last *old* word that has been spoken. Life, including our life with our German neighbours, must go on; it will go on, and it will go on from the point where we now confront them. We have followed, as on one of our mountain paths, a long straight course

THE ONLY WAY

to the last stage; if we want to go further, as we must, then we must go round the bend and higher —not back to where our eyes were blind to what we now see, nor yet further in the direction in which, with our eyes at last opened, we took the last step, that is, not further in the feeling we so rightly have of deep repugnance and repudiation of the Germans today.

It was high time that we felt a deep and serious indignation. But there can be no such righteous wrath upon which we could dare to let the sun go down. Even the French and the Dutch, the Norwegians and the Poles, even the Jews throughout the world will one day have to be clear about that. It is very much more difficult for them than it is for us. But we, who have hardly been directly touched by the German evil, and do not need to call for vengeance on the Germans for anything or anyone, need to sweep our own doorsteps and tell ourselves that it befits us to be among the first to be clear about it. We must go round the bend. To bring this to pass is my concern in this essay.

I

I begin with a very simple but by no means self-evident proposition: in any case we *know* too little of the Germans of today to be able to "have done" with them once and for all.

What we do know of them is what we have gradually, from all sides, and with terrifying precision and clarity, learned from their actions since the beginning of the Hitler régime and especially in the course of this war. In war and in peace, there have always and everywhere been lies and slavery, brutality and great outbreaks of such inhumanity as cries to heaven. We must certainly not forget that our own ancestors, who for the rest, and with right, are highly extolled, were, in their very time of martial splendour, not in the least angelic. But the Germany of today—and this distinguishes it also from revolutionary Russia—has raised inhumanity to a principle, a system and a method. National-Socialism is not only bound up but also identical with inhumanity. All theoretical objections of this order which were formerly raised against its thoughts and teachings have been far surpassed by its practice; for meantime by its practice it has with an ever increasing clarity shown its true nature and (one may assuredly add) condemned itself. It is repugnant to me to rehearse, let alone to expatiate on the endless sequence of what the National-Socialists and thus the Germans have done. We know well enough. And it is overwhelmingly what has been done first in Germany itself, and later wherever the Germans established their authority, which have alienated us from them.

But we must reflect: we know enough—more than enough—about what the Germans have done; but we know very little, in fact almost nothing, of the Germans themselves, of the *German people*, of the extent or nature or sense in which they have or have not shared in these actions and are or are not responsible for them. Do we know whether there were few or many—perhaps very many—who opposed these actions from the very beginning—while Britain still slept, while we too slept? Do we know the sincerity and determination, even the partial success, with which that opposition may have persisted? Do we know where the German worker, the German peasant, the German minister, the German woman, really stand today and where they have to be sought? What did those Swiss women know of the German soldiers whom they spat upon in the open street?

THE ONLY WAY

We cannot indeed reflect too much upon what it means that for the last twelve years something like an iron curtain has been dropped between the German people and ourselves. We have not been able to look into their eyes or hear them speak for themselves. No free and open word has reached us from across the German frontier. Their newspapers and books tell us at best how much must be continually suppressed and avoided. Their letters, so far as they reach us, can tell us precisely nothing of what is important for us to know in order to understand them. The German people wear, at least for us, a mask like the medieval lepers. We are seeing the machinery of that system in full swing. We see that opposition to it by word and deed, which certainly was and is present here and there, has at least till now not been effective. We see that millions upon millions of German men and women, young and old, are continually more or less actively engaged in keeping this machine going and thereby continually making possible new and fateful German deeds. But let us not deceive ourselves: in all this we have not yet seen the German people. At best we all know *some* of them, but the German of today we do not know. It is part of the present German evil, there is perhaps even an element of abnormality in the German inhumanity, that the situation is as it is, and that the two are separated in such ghostly fashion—the German actions and system and machine which we know, and the German himself, whom in fact we no longer know, who is, it may be, just what his doings seem to show, yet, it may also be, is not in the least what his doings seem to show.

We should like to know, and we ought to know, if what the present spokesmen of the German people, who are at the same time its bitterest enemies, assert is really true—namely, that the overwhelming majority of this people has desired and explicitly and tacitly approved and in its heart is in sympathy with what has been done for twelve years in its name. Alternatively, we should like to know, and we ought to know, if the reverse is true, as the "Free Germany" of General Von Seydlitz from Moscow, or wherever it may be, assures us— namely, that the overwhelming majority of this people is itself but the first and most lamentable victim of that machine, and must never be held responsible for the German actions which dominate the picture today. Which is the correct version? Or is a third version correct, which claims that the German is in a quite peculiar way a being with two completely different mentalities, so that in every German one would have to look simultaneously for something of Friedrich Schiller and Matthias Claudius as well as something of Joseph Goebbels and Heinrich Himmler, something of the spirit of Weimar as well as of the spirit of Potsdam? But over and above all that, there seems to be something like a spirit—represented by not a few Germans—of Oradour and Oswiecim.[1]

Which of these is the true German spirit? There are arguments and circumstantial evidence pointing each way. We have been constantly hearing of individuals and of whole groups, Communists, Bible students, Roman Catholics, students, officers, also of convinced Protestants, who resisted in word and deed and have paid for it with their lives. We might some day stand amazed and ashamed on learning that very much more had happened and had been suffered in this way, perhaps in this very hour is happening and is being suffered, than we ever dreamed. Our picture of the German of today would then have once more to undergo a radical revision.

I for my part am convinced that this will be the case. But I cannot prove it today. We know very little now of the strength of this resistance within

---

[1] *Oswiecim*—a concentration camp in Poland. *Oradour-sur-Glane*—a French village which was destroyed, and the inhabitants shot or burned, on June 10, 1944. A full description of the incident was reported in *The Times* of July 14, 1944.

Germany. We do not know a thing, for example, of what our friend Martin Niemoeller has been really thinking about this war and with what political views he will finally, if he is spared to us, emerge from his prison. Are there not even German Jews who to this day are not wholly weaned from some kind of conditional adherence to National-Socialism, or to the German policy of which the pattern was created by Bismarck, from which National-Socialism has developed with little deviation? Can the Germans, should the Germans, be trusted anew today? We are urgently summoned to do this. On the other hand we are just as urgently warned against it. But the foundation of the summons and the foundation of the warning are alike hidden in darkness. If we bring together all that we know and do not know then we shall have to conclude that no one can act as if he had quite authentic information on either side about the German of today.

I should like to cast a quick glance now at the different *theories* by which the German of today is usually explained.

It is said, for example, that in National-Socialism we are dealing with the explosive outbreak of a primeval savage layer of consciousness, and to some extent with a revelation of the primitive man

THE ONLY WAY

whom modern civilized man has only apparently overcome, and whom he has to some extent provoked by the sophisticated soullessness of his progress in civilization. It is said, that is, that we are dealing with a psychological or rather a psychopathic reaction in which modern man was caught and in which he could create a breathing-space for himself only by such a destructive—moreover such a profoundly self-destructive—undertaking. It is in some such dark direction that Rauschning's book, *Germany's Revolution of Destruction,* has pointed.

But there are also theories which move in more intelligible regions. To think of a German is to think of a Prussian; to think of a Prussian is to think of the Prussian military drill. It is recalled that the German people has never really got rid of princes, that it has never had the opportunity of seeing in the State anything but an instrument for giving orders, that it has been spiritually educated, especially by the Lutheran Reformation, to accept precisely such a state of affairs without variation. National-Socialism is then very simply explained as the supreme blossoming of this passion, which has become second nature to the German, for dictatorship and servility, of the German desire to command and to obey, of the German longing for authority and disposition to subordination.

Another explanation is as follows. The capitalist economic crisis at the end of the twenties and beginning of the thirties threatened to lead in Germany to a revolutionary rising of the working classes. In this situation the apprehensive German capitalists thought they saw in Hitler a possible deliverer, and secured him as their *condottiere*. The industrialists and the bank-magnates gave him money, with which he organized his astonishing party, mustered and armed his brown and black armies, till at last he outgrew his masters. Then, thanks to the strength of his demagogy and the weakness of the democratic government which was itself infected with capitalist and fascist tendencies, thanks to the prevailing unemployment and the divided German working class, he came to power. According to this theory all the abominations of National-Socialism are nothing but the vices of the capitalist economic system developed to their proper conclusion and revealing their real character.

Yet another variant is the Germans' own self-pitying account and justification of their aberrations. They are, they say, the nation which arrived too late on the scene of history and up till now has

THE ONLY WAY

come off badly, the "young nation," the "nation without living space" in the centre of Europe, which on account of its qualities is on every side hated and grudged a place in the sun. It is because they were driven by necessity to take action against the threat of this encirclement that they have become, were positively forced to become, what we see them to be today.

One of the most remarkable theories about the Germans is undoubtedly that of their old enemy from the last war, the French president Clemenceau. I quote it in his own words, as he gave it to his private secretary shortly before his death.

"Dear friend," he said, "it is man's nature to love life. The German does not know this cult. In the German soul, in the art and thought and literature of this people there is a kind of insensibility to all that life really means, to what makes its fascination and its grandeur. Instead they have a sickly and satanic love of death. These people love death. These people cherish a divinity on whom they look with trembling and yet with a smiling ecstasy which renders them completely unbalanced. And this God is death. Whence is this derived? I know no answer to that question. The German adores war out of self-love and because at its end there is the assurance of carnage. War is a contract with death. The German meets death as if it were the mistress dearest to his heart."

Besides all these there is another theory, with a Christian reference. It is that the Germans are possessed of the real meaning of Christianity and have understood the grace of God, in the person of the Jew, Jesus, more deeply and fundamentally than any other people. For this very reason they, and they alone, have been capable of such thorough-going and logical repudiation of Jesus, his people, and his message, as they have now brought to completion in their political and military practice from Frederick the Great through Bismarck to Hitler. It is for this reason that they, and they alone, have been capable of that criminal and cold contempt for mankind which is characteristic of these national heroes.

One and all, these theories are open to question. I shall not pause to criticize them in detail. Undoubtedly they all contain much that is worth notice and reflection, but it is perhaps worth remarking that none of them has the character of a revelation. None of them explains why it is precisely in Germany that these phenomena and their respective consequences should appear. It would therefore be a good thing if the advocates of these various explanations were to institute comparisons

THE ONLY WAY

at least of one with another, supplementing each with the others, without assuming that any one of these hypotheses exhausts all the information available about the German people. How great must be the enigma of Germany when it evokes so many and such conflicting solutions! The German as he has become and as he lives today, with all that he has behind him of good and evil, good fortune and bad, hopes and disillusionments, may in large measure correspond to what these theories say of him and yet his situation may be quite different. We must test them, in the hope that with their help we may make some approach to the German enigma. But this must not prevent us from keeping an open mind, in spite of all the theories, towards the real German as he will meet us when one day the iron curtain goes up again.

We have to look forward to this meeting without any optimistic illusions. It may be that everything is much as is now supposed. It may even be that everything is much worse. And we can really promise no one that he will find the Germans more congenial after this than before. It may even be—indeed for my own part I am convinced of it—that we shall have to marshal our information and draw our conclusions in an atmosphere quite different from any we can now imagine.

THE ONLY WAY

At this stage I want simply to draw attention to the fact that this is possible and that we must keep our minds open for it. My own view is that we should reserve for ourselves the same liberty of outlook in relation to the equally enigmatic problem of Soviet Russia. It would be not at all good for us, when we reach the end of the great conflict now taking place, and stand in the morning of the new day, to be among those who think they have the key to the riddle of the nations in their private possession. With all that we now know, and with all the certainty of the convictions we have formed in these recent years, we must still be ready to see other nations afresh, as they will present themselves to us in the forms they have taken in these same years. It is this open-mindedness which we simply must not abandon now, even in regard to the Germans. There are pessimistic as well as optimistic illusions.

II

We are on quite different ground, on which we can move with relatively greater assurance, when we now ask, further, in what kind of material condition we shall find the Germans when we are able to see them once again.

It is more than a mere supposition to say that it will resemble nothing so much as the condition of Carthage or Jerusalem after their destruction. It will certainly not be this time as after the last war, when it was possible for Germany, in spite of her defeat, to enjoy a measure of prosperity after a relatively short time; when old and young—I experienced it at close quarters from 1921 onwards—found time, energy and leisure enough to turn passionately and at once to the question of new martial glories for Germany; and when a new and unprecedented programme of military, economic and technical re-armament could be carried through comparatively soon.

This time the Germans have not only terror without end but they also have asked for and had imposed on them this end with terror. The end has

THE ONLY WAY

in large measure begun already. Their complaint that their opponents are about to overcome them with the superiority of their mechanized material comes too late; for it was they who first—and for a time successfully enough—appealed to this very power. They sought to subject everybody and everything to compulsion; now they are themselves subject to compulsion as no other nation has been within the memory of man. They sought to obliterate the cities of others, and they did so as long as they could; now it is their own cities which are being even more thoroughly laid in ruins. They drove whole nations from their hearths and homes; now millions of their own people are in flight from the west to the east and from east to west. They ran amok in every direction under heaven, slaying and slaying; now what waves of irreparable destruction have swept through the ranks of their own men and youths and boys. They invoked the spirits and the spirits came. And the end is not yet.

One thing is certain, that with the passing of the sign of the swastika the German eagle will also pass. It is sometimes doubtful whether even the German refugees are quite clear about this. It will no longer be a question of any particular kind of German glory, but only, in terrible and unambiguous conditions of hardship, a question of German

THE ONLY WAY

life. For apart from anything else confidence on the part of other nations is requisite before they will permit a nation to enjoy power, to become a Great Power and a leading power. Germany enjoyed this confidence once; but not now. Ever since she gained power she has misused it, first of all in a dubious and finally in an intolerable fashion. Without a doubt this power must be taken from her, and will be taken; and that not only to protect others from her, but also to protect herself. The achievement of Frederick the Great and Bismarck could not be brought to a more logical conclusion nor to more complete destruction than it has been done by Adolf Hitler. It is indeed possible that the German state and German unity have been disposed of for a long time. One thinks almost with horror of the German fairy tale—if only they had remembered it in Germany in time!—of the fisherman who, invited by an enchanted prince, in the guise of a fish he had caught, to express his wishes, asked at the instigation of his wife Ilsebill first of all for a hut to live in, then for a stone house, then for a castle, then for a king's throne, then for the Emperor's throne, all of which he received in due order, until finally, wishing to be the Lord God himself, he was returned to the pigsty from which he had emerged.

THE ONLY WAY

These years have been hard for the other nations as well. They too have bled and suffered; even we Swiss have had to bear certain hardships. But it is one thing to be able to say that the effort and the sacrifice have not been in vain, and have served a good or at least a necessary purpose; it is quite another thing to face the fact that in a destructive and vain undertaking, for the sake of sheer folly and wickedness and with a purely negative result, so much has been done, so much undergone and sacrificed. And the recognition of this fact is what awaits the German people, as soon as they are again capable of the slightest self-examination. The other nations, including ourselves, will certainly enter the post-war period heavy-laden with anxiety. But it is one thing to face the future with certain tangible hopes and prospects as well as with one's cares; it is quite another thing to be, so to speak, reduced to zero, to have simply nothing to work on, simply no idea of how things will go on or what form they will take. This is what awaits the Germans. It is quite unthinkable how radically they will be at an end and have to start afresh with the most rudimentary beginnings, once everything is over and done. No; this time they will have to wait long and patiently for the most essential elements of recovery. This time it will certainly not be

THE ONLY WAY

so easy to reach back past the bad yesterday to a better day-before-yesterday. This time even the memory of the valour of the German Army—doubtless proved anew—will not be able to bring this war retrospectively into a transfiguring light. This time no romantically inspired youth will wander with guitar and song through the German countryside as though nothing had happened, to be changed by sleight of hand into another dangerous warrior horde. This time the German burgher, the German professor and the German student will not so quickly find their way back to the old paths. This time even the finest German efficiency and eloquence will be unable to bluff the world again, and so quickly. This time, thanks to what has intervened, too much has been laid low, rendered superfluous and problematic and impossible. Both the external pressure on the body of the German nation and its inevitable inner convulsions will be too great. The new Germany, however things may take shape, will be a land full of sadness. In the *Colloquies* of Erasmus of Rotterdam there is a passage which runs *Videtis iam inverti mundi scenam. Aut deponenda est persona aut agendae sunt suae cuique partes.* "The scene of the world changes. Either you take your exit, or you play the part allotted to you." The German

THE ONLY WAY

people will not take its exit from the stage of the world. But the scene has changed. The part it must play for a long time will be a very modest and painful one.

What does it all mean for us? I should like above all to emphasize that we should count ourselves fortunate that we do not have to share in the judgment that is now of necessity breaking over the Germans. It is undoubtedly a good thing, for which we Swiss have to thank our neutrality, that we do not share in the difficult responsibility of the victors, that we do not have to make a decision about what is now to become of Germany, and how her internal and external relations, once everything is over, have to be ordered. But this must certainly include our complete abstention from the triumph, the satisfaction and the gloating of those who always knew better, who were always right. Enough stones will be cast at the dying and dead lion without our joining in. Of course we breathe more freely as the hour of settlement arrives. And what I should like to recommend as our attitude is not just the transition from fear to pity. After Germany's defeat in the last war, the whole world, including ourselves, took things too easily: all at once we were filled with pity, and the Germans made use of that for thoroughly bad ends. Since we are

THE ONLY WAY

destined to be spectators, it is fitting that we should at least be *genuine* spectators of this *genuine* tragedy.

There is a text in the Old Testament in which may be recognized almost word for word what is now happening and will happen to Germany. It is in the fourteenth chapter of the prophet Isaiah, where there is a song about the fall of the King of Babylon, whose most vigorous passage contains the famous words:

*How art thou fallen from heaven, O Lucifer, son
 of the morning!
How art thou cut down to the ground, which didst
 weaken the nations!
For thou hast said in thine heart, I will ascend into
 heaven,
I will exalt my throne above the stars of God:
I will sit also upon the mount of the congregation,
 in the sides of the North:
I will ascend above the heights of the clouds;
I will be like the most High.
Yet thou shalt be brought down to hell, to the
 sides of the pit.*

A song of triumph? So it is called, unfortunately, in German editions. Yes; it certainly does not show pity, it certainly shows triumph, but the triumph is veiled by something quite different, by a deep sympathy with what is described, by a deep awe which at the same time helps him who has been stricken down, who from such a height has fallen so low.

This is how we should look at the Germans when they appear before us again—deeply moved, with sympathy, with awe. We should look at them like this even when we cannot help agreeing that things were in justice bound to end this way, even when we cannot wish that this war might have a different conclusion. We should judge ourselves if now, when everything is happening before our very eyes as it was bound to happen, we were able to avoid this deep emotion and sympathy and awe. In deep emotion we shall watch the end of the Germany as she has been till now, when the knowledge dawns upon us that we too are concerned in this end; for it is a sign of the immovable limit, set not only to the German nature, but also to all human nature, including our own, in its qualities and its defects, a sign of the eternal law which will break man if he does not bend before it. But in sympathy too? Yes, in sympathy too: for the lightning has struck the earth so near us and could easily have struck us as well. When we see another

THE ONLY WAY

broken on that eternal law then something is bound to break in us as well. Who could rejoice in *Der Nibelunge Not* without suffering at the same time? In the visible and palpable disturber of the peace are we not bound to recognize ourselves as only slightly less visible and palpable disturbers of the peace, in the judgment he is now undergoing something that we too have fundamentally deserved?

But in awe as well? Yes, really in awe as well. How could we not bow before the situation in which another has had, however justly, every support struck away, and in which nothing, nothing at all, seems to be left to him but to start afresh, in the most difficult circumstances and conditions, to break up the fallow ground? Might one not for a moment think almost with envy of this situation which is so desperate but also so uniquely promising? A whole people seems to be so rarely given even the opportunity to start afresh. To be able to start afresh: what a task, what a possibility, if it were utilized! What a rare distinction above the ninety-nine righteous, to receive even the opportunity! We have not climbed so high as the Germans, so obviously we have not fallen so low. Happy we! For that very reason no such opportunity is extended to us. We do not know what the Germans will make of it. But we cannot really think without awe and expectation of the fact that the question of existence has now been so radically put to them. We cannot help wondering whether, being now the last, they might not some day become, in a quite different sense, the first.

This, then, is the second thing asked of us—especially as we look at Germany's present fate: at all costs, as the end draws near, we must think of them across the frontier with this deep emotion and sympathy and awe. But let there be no misunderstanding: we must do this without for a moment forgetting or denying what our attitude to the German question had to be, and has to remain till this end is reached. If our attitude was genuine and right, and if it remains so till the end, then when the end does come (and it is not far off today), it must acquire this new character.

III

We now reach the question—what do we owe the Germans to-day? We must not turn this question into the quite different question of what they deserve. Not even their enemies, let alone us, are required to say what they deserve. What we owe them is quite independent of what they deserve. What we owe them is determined rather by what they *need* and what we can give and be to them. And what the Germans need now, at the dark turning-point of their way, is, quite simply, *friends*. They have made enemies enough and now they have them; they have to be terribly alone now, ringed round by enemies; in precisely the way in which, in better days—dramatizing their life and condition without rhyme or reason—they depicted it often enough to themselves and to others. Now matters have really gone so far that they have only enemies and no friends. What they need, then, is sure friends, and what we owe them is to be their friends. A man is another's friend when he is not against him but *for* him. Everything else in friendship follows indirectly from this direct relation. Let us try to understand what it means in this connection.

A friend is, above all, something other than a teacher. I am saying nothing against teachers; I am a teacher myself. But a teacher sits at his desk, teaches what he knows and what his pupils do not know, sets tasks and listens, gives marks and writes reports. A teacher simply cannot help being, in fact, in some solid measure, *against* his pupil and, therefore, not his friend. From the pupil's point of view, at any rate—and that is what counts—that is certainly how it looks. If the teacher wanted to be the pupil's friend, then he would have to do something very unlike a teacher: he would have to leave his desk, become the pupil's companion, and thus cease to be his teacher.

Now we Swiss are by nature a nation of teachers, and the great danger with regard to the Germans is that when the time comes we should want most of all to sit behind our desks. That would be a great misfortune. In the United States they are supposed to be all ready to deliver after the war a whole cargo of teaching facilities to Germany, in order to inculcate in the barbarians (after so much Wotan Worship, nihilism and rifle-practice) human brotherhood, democracy, respect for law, love

THE ONLY WAY

of peace and (instead of the vile *Horst Wessel Lied*), *Onward Christian Soldiers*. The intention is admirable, but it can never work. The Germans, however bad their state, will retreat into themselves, like an oyster into its shell, before all who approach them as teachers, and German youth will defend itself against them tooth and nail. They will treat all who approach them in the guise of teachers as people who are *against* them, and much more against them than those who came earlier in aircraft and tanks. What the Germans need is friends; real friends, and not such friends as Job had. Job's friends, too, were in their way excellent men. They had only one fault, that they wanted to be his teachers, not his friends, and once behind their desks they never climbed down. What we owe the Germans is that we should be their real and sincere friends.

But that would mean being unconditionally *for* them and not *against* them. Unconditionally means without waiting for their conversion, without the reservation that they must first become congenial to us, that they must first better themselves and become different, that they must be given moral instruction until they respond to treatment and we can be for them. It means that we are not to put them on probation and we are not to be anxious about being duped again; it simply means being ready to make their concern our own.

What the Germans have always secretly lacked and will lack today to a frightful extent, is the belief that man can be man's friend, that he can be unconditionally for him instead of against him, that such a thing does exist in the world. The other nations, including ourselves, believe in such a possibility—at any rate we think and say we do. In Anglo-Saxon religious terminology, no words are more fondly cherished than "fellowship" and "community," and we in Switzerland have the equally fine word *Genossenschaft*. The Germans lack the ear for these words. Put in another way, what the Germans have always lacked and what they must get along without now is a firm grip of what forgiveness is; that men can be for one another in spite of the fact that they have much against one another which they cannot overlook and forget. That this apparently intimate Christian possibility of forgiveness is both strong in itself and the deepest wisdom of a strong policy, has always seemed to the Germans to be a Utopian thought, although the sober and practical and successful use the English made of it in South Africa and elsewhere must have stared them in the face. They know no other politics but power politics.

THE ONLY WAY

But what the Germans need is not that those fine words should be preached at them. They have a deep and ancient mistrust of those words; one can even say that they are fervent unbelievers in them. They imagine that sheer hypocritical self-seeking lies behind them. And, in fact, the other nations, including us Swiss, have not yet succeeded in making these words clear and impressive and credible to them. Again and again they have considered a solid and threatening hostility of man to man and nation to nation to be the more honourable and certain basis of life. They are unable to have a full belief in anything but hostility. When German theologians talk of God as the "Lord of History," and when Hitler invokes the "Almighty" or "Providence," they are thinking of war as the final wisdom and father of all things. It is senseless to become indignant or excited about it. They assert that this is all they have encountered in the world. "The solidarity of the nations has never been a political reality for them." (W. Schubart). In this belief they set out to the strains of the Hohenfriedberg March, on the way to where in the end the *Horst Wessel Lied* was to sound, and which has led them to this frightful point where their guilt turns into the destiny which it has summoned. In this situation it would not help them in the least

THE ONLY WAY

for us to preach those fine words to them. They would have to see that these words are true, and they can only see this if we so approach them that their truth can be seen and heard, tasted and felt on their own bodies. They would have to experience friendship, not the friendship of Job's comforters, but real and sincere friendship.

The Russians, the English, the Americans, the French and the smaller nations so badly treated by the Germans, together with the Jews, cannot be expected at this moment to offer them such a friendship, although they, too, will one day have to see that the German peril can be finally and decisively removed only in this way. But it is to be expected of us Swiss, because we are Swiss and because (I must now make express use of the presupposition) we are *Christian* Swiss.

What the Germans have to see in us is that we know how to ask and how to answer, in all sobriety and not in accordance with our own interest, the question, *Who is my neighbour?* It is possible that in itself friendship with the English, for example, or the Russians, whose best aspects we have come to know in these recent years, would interest us much more. But the question at present is whether we are ready to be friends with those who *need* us. What the Germans have to see in us is that in

THE ONLY WAY

Switzerland we understand Christianity to mean first the Gospel and only after that the Law. With the Law—including the moral and social law—in the forefront of our thoughts, we can only be their teachers and, therefore, against them. With the Gospel in the forefront and in our hearts we could be, we would have to be their friends, and unconditionally for them; not for some kind of ideal Germans or some future kind of better Germans, but for the real Germans of to-day in all the shame of the National-Socialism scourings with which we see them besmeared.

For Jesus Christ is also for them, and, moreover, unconditionally for them. And let there be no misunderstanding about this: He is for us in no different way than He is for them. By calling us His friends, He takes into the bargain the particular shame with which we are besmeared. If we should try to justify ourselves, and say that such unconditioned friendship is too much to ask of us with regard to the Germans, then, however good our arguments, we should consider well whether the cry of Jesus Christ, *Come unto me, all ye that labour and are heavy laden,* instead of travelling through us to the Germans, might not reach them without touching us and without having any meaning for us. Once more I recall the unique opportunity now offered to them. "Come unto me, you unlikeable ones, you wicked Hitler boys and girls, you brutal S.S. soldiers, you evil Gestapo police, you sad compromisers and collaborationists, all you men of the herd who have moved so long in patient stupidity behind your so-called leader. Come unto me, you guilty and you accomplices, who now obtain your deserts, as you were bound to do. Come unto me, I know you well, but I do not ask who you are and what you have done, I see only that you have reached the end and must start afresh, for good or ill; I will refresh you, I will start afresh from zero with you. If these Swiss, swollen with the democratic and social and Christian ideas which they have always extolled, are not interested in you, I am interested. If they do not wish to say to you, then I say to you 'I am for you, I am your friend'." What if they should hear that to our exclusion? What if the German chance became the supreme Swiss mischance, if the fate of the Pharisee was fulfilled in us—the Pharisee who had every possible excellence, who was undoubtedly a good teacher as well, but of whom this one good thing could not be said—that he "went down to his house justified." At this point I feel greater anxiety for our own way than for the Germans' way. Can we strike the way that must be taken here?

THE ONLY WAY

For our own sakes we should not refuse to be the real and sincere friends of the Germans today.

I shall interpolate some remarks here about the "Swiss Fund" and the special relief for foreign churches in distress. For a long time one could see with a certain anxiety the moment approaching when we would have in large measure paid the price for our fortunate preservation in this war, and at the same time set the crown on our proven virtue by appearing amongst the other nations as the charitable and beneficent Swiss. I do not know if this role—of being the "capital city of the world's philanthropy"—fine though it is, will in the long run do us good. At any rate we shall not make any real sacrifices when we consider the luxury spending which is still possible to us; what we can give, in face of the depth of the present need, means no more than a drop in a bucket; or must we conceal from ourselves the fact that in this matter we are also acting in our own interests. But that is neither here nor there. There can be no question that whatever we can do will benefit those it reaches. But it must have nothing to do with giving marks and prizes according to our own estimate, however justified it may be. The person who differentiates, who wants to give, but not for the Germans, should rather give nothing and realize that he simply does not know what giving means in the present situation. This is a practical test of whether our Swiss readiness to help is in the last resort an honourable thing or not. This is where the immediate decision is reached today of whether we shall be capable or incapable of the free and unreserved attitude towards the Germans which I have already described. No; it *cannot* be that we shall remain hard when once the Germans and the German need appear clearly before our eyes.

Last autumn, there was a picture in our illustrated papers of German women, children and old men, leaving the blitzed town of Aachen, with the few possessions they had saved, and in the foreground, clutching his heavily-laden mother by the hand, was a four-year old child with a great white flag over his shoulders: the present German question, the present German need in bodily form. Yes, we say, we see that, of course; but we have also before our eyes the towns and villages of others, blitzed and plundered and laid waste by the Germans. Who began it? Who now receives payment for what he has done a hundredfold to others? If that was a French or Italian child, we would be taking good note of the white flag of surrender, we would certainly say to ourselves that now we must help where we can. But it is a German child. Who

THE ONLY WAY

knows what a Nazi his father may have been? And have we not heard in what devilries (for instance, in the kind of evening prayers they are taught) the children, the very youngest children, were brought up in Germany, and how those same poor German boys, who were welcomed and cherished in Norway in 1920, returned in 1940 as enemy soldiers who knew the land? Quite right—and quite wrong. These and the like are precisely the kind of thoughts we ought *not* to think at present, whether in connection with the Swiss Fund or with anything else. These thoughts are quite right, but they are not those of friends, nor do they make for friendship; and because the Germans in their qualities and defects now need friends, because we owe it to them to be friendly, such thoughts must be *impossible* to us at present. If we want to do something to enable the Germans to spare themselves and us a third world war, we must meet them with a *pure* heart and therefore must think of them *now* with a pure heart.

But we have not quite said all that has to be said at this point. It is well known that it is a property of sincere friendship to be able to *contradict* the other and to contradict him in the most definite way, if one sees that he needs it for his own sake.

THE ONLY WAY

We can and ought to meet the Germans—let us meet them—with the words: "Strengthen the things which remain, that are ready to die." We can help them, we must help them, so far as the power lies in us, to start afresh in a new Germany—no longer as the *Herrenvolk* which, immediately after the last war, and in the end more wildly than ever before, they longed to become, nor as the nation of gladiators and slaves which, strangely enough, they were bound to become in the carrying out of their purpose, but, in complete rejection of that disastrous idea, as a *free* people. We can perhaps impart to them the spirit and the desire to become a really mature people from now on, living without the swastika or the eagle. We can perhaps advise and help them from new and most modest beginnings to become politically reasonable, healthy, and fit for life. We can draw their attention to the fact that in their own history there have existed blighted and suppressed rudiments of a structure of a quite different kind, to which they might now return and which they might now honour. We can show our sympathy to those of the Germans today who desire such a reconstruction, and we can stretch out our hand to them. And we can raise our voices before the whole world in favour of their being given—with all the needful circumspection and foresight—the necessary chance for such an enterprise.

Of course, we could not help them to justify and excuse and build up again, under whatever name, the Germany that has been. The more thoroughly that Germany is unbuilt, the better—above all for themselves. We could not help them to escape the expiation and restitution and complete re-orientation that are now necessary. We could not help them in any attempt to return to the ways which have led them to the point reached today. You may often hear it said, in connection with the appeal for the distressed churches abroad, that we shall have to help them in accordance with their own wishes. True enough; but we shall for heaven's sake not have to help the German churches to be built up again in the style and spirit they have had till now. In sincere friendship we cannot do that, precisely because we know that the old Germany is lost—and the Church authorities and the theological faculties have played so far a fateful role in this old Germany. It is lost because it was a thoroughly bad thing, so that the Germans would only continue to do themselves harm if they tried to take it up again. Long live the Germans! But what has been done in Germany must now be replaced by something quite different. With all due regard for the historical background, the person who is sincerely for the Germans will have to be as hard as iron towards them, at any sign of a retrogression.

It will certainly not be easy to be their sincere friend in this respect. It will not be easy to make clear to them that we mean them well, that we are turning to them without conditions, that we want to meet them not as the Pharisee did the publican, and that nevertheless, in this respect, we cannot yield them an inch. We must indeed love them very much if we are not to run away from this task but take it up properly. The difficulty is enormous. For it is by no means self-evident that even now the Germans themselves will understand so easily that old things have passed away, that they must "break up their fallow ground," and therefore *dare* not sow among thorns.

We have to reckon with the possibility that the great majority of Germans even now scarcely realize in what collective madness they have lived so long, with what deep-seated and justifiable consternation Germany is regarded, what a responsibility they assumed when they supported first Bismarck, then Wilhelm II, and last of all, Adolf Hitler, and willingly and patiently did all they were told; and that especially they have no inkling of

THE ONLY WAY

the horror and loathing with which the German name has been surrounded in the last twelve years. It will be difficult to persuade them even to see the facts and to admit them.

But something else must be reckoned with—the remarkable German quality of living down in the grand manner all unpleasant memories, and twisting them into their opposite. That the story of the re-establishment of the German *Reich* by Bismarck was a story of lies and violence was known very well by millions of Germans when it happened, namely between 1860 and 1870; and they showed their indignation clearly enough at the time. Twenty years later all that was forgotten, and a single heroic story had grown out of it. This quality might come into play again now.

We have further to reckon with the fact that the Germans love to meet every political accusation with an immediate counter-accusation and with indignant counter-claims. Thus, in Germany, the recognition of the last war as an attempt at least to hazard an honourable struggle with democracy was straightway obliterated and rendered impossible by a flood of invective against the Versailles Treaty. So now some new saga or other could be launched in Germany, according to which the English, the Russians, the whole world—but not the

Germans themselves—would be responsible for the present calamity, and according to which it would be the Germans above all who were entitled to claim and demand all sorts of things from the rest.

We have further to reckon with the historico-philosophical profundity of the Germans. They have an excessive love of interpreting themselves, now as the executors, now as the victims of great historical necessities fraught with destiny, and it is clear that from that standpoint, too, it will be difficult for them to become properly sober again and reach a healthy state of responsible thought and sound insights and really free decisions.

Finally, we must reckon with the religious profundity of the Germans, which all too willingly avoids the acknowledgement of their own concrete guilt by pointing out the great truth that before God in the last resort all men and nations are alike guilty and alike need forgiveness for their sins: thus the bold conclusion is drawn that a particular German repentance is obviously unnecessary and absolutely uncalled for.

From each of these points a path leads backwards which the Germans can under no circumstances be allowed to follow. Therefore, on each of these points, they must be resisted—in all friendship, in all patience (and the Germans can make one impatient!) and without faltering: not in order to extort a confession of sin from them, which in fact they do not owe us, but in order to give them the opportunity to look and move really forwards and not to turn back, and in order that we may be able to live and work with them on good solid ground. Everything depends on their finding us perfectly free from sentimentality, and (through our being not against them but for them), on our having nothing to do with any line of thought, however impressive, which includes any appeal in a case already settled. We must in future not let ourselves be imposed upon by the great German art of intellectual evasion—not only for our own sake, but also for the sake of the Germans themselves; least of all if we mean them well.

Everything would depend, then, on its being made absolutely clear to them that we do not stand where they have stood so long, and that our friendship contains the invitation to them to betake themselves in a quite different direction. But this invitation can be truly inviting only if we have made it clear to them from the start that we are not their enemies but their friends, who mean them well. All is lost if we meet them in Pharisaic fashion. We would have to steer a middle course between Pharisaism and sentimentality. That is what makes the task so difficult. To be Pharisaic is easy; to be sentimental is also easy. But it is difficult to be at once quite ready for everything and quite firm, quite soft and quite hard. I do not need to describe how near we shall be every moment to drifting to the one side or the other. I have nothing to say if someone should object that in what I have described as the kind of friendship we need to extend to the Germans we are dealing with something rather like a squaring of the circle. But I do not know how, when everything is taken into account, we could describe in any other way what is demanded of us. What the Germans need now is sincere friendship in this *double* sense. And that is what we owe them.

IV

We have said a great deal about the Germans, but very little about ourselves, and we must now make this good. This may at the same time serve as an answer to the very pressing question whether we can or cannot give the Germans what we owe them.

Let us imagine that a German has been listening to what I have said so far. Let us suppose he is neither arrogant nor narrow-minded. Let us, therefore, imagine that he would not try to settle us by saying that in the whole thing he had only heard our "No," our objection to all that was great and important to him as a German; that we are inveterate enemies of the Reich, and now have topped all by obviously succumbing to Anglo-Saxon propaganda; and so on and on. Let us imagine, further, that he would not try to crush us by explaining that even in the event of their bitterest defeat, the Germans would always be a great nation, while we Swiss would always be a modest nation of four million people, and that it was a boundless exaggeration of our own impor-

THE ONLY WAY

tance to suppose that the Germans would ever attach much weight for good or for evil to whatever attitude we adopted towards them. Let us not imagine such a one, but a thoroughly educated German, and let us suppose he answers me as follows:

"My dear Swiss, I have heard that you are racking your brains about how you should think of us and behave towards us. I understand that you have much against us and that we have wearied you with our iniquities. I herewith inform you that I know we are hard to understand. I make no claim to glory for that, as we have so often done. I confess, rather, that I am entirely of your opinion about all that has incidentally been said against us. I know that we have erred and strayed from our ways, that now we must take the consequences and, as you say, begin again from zero. In future, God willing, no responsible German will allow that saying to pass his lips, which is in every conceivable way arrogant and senseless, that Germany will be the saviour of the world. I know that for us there is only one interesting question, and that is, whether, and how, in the end, Germany itself may be saved. This I know and confess. And I understand, too, that you are honestly labouring to overcome a purely negative attitude to us, and to be our friends once again. I herewith inform you that I am thankful to you for this honest desire, because we indeed need friends, and that I wish you well in your effort. So much for that.

"But, my dear Swiss, what is your authority for all this—for your concern about us, for your criticism of us, for your offer to us which you are struggling at long last to make. 'The Germans and ourselves'—How dare you Swiss, how dare you personally, Professor Karl Barth, as Swiss, confront us, as Germans, in this way about which we have just heard? What if I as a German were now to announce a lecture on the subject 'The Swiss and ourselves'? And understand me aright, please: not from my high horse, not beginning with Bismarck or Hitler, but just from that zero which we have now reached and where, when all is over, we shall stand in the sight of all. What if I were then to make the following points?

"From 1933 onwards, and till very recently, you have laid the greatest emphasis on maintaining not only correct, but actually friendly, relations—not with the German people, but with the Hitler régime. You were in the greatest haste to acknowledge *de jure*—mark well, *de jure*—the misdeeds of our Hitler's boon companions, Franco and Mussolini. You looked askance on the fugitive opponents of the Hitler régime; at that time you wanted to know very little about international democratic solidarity. And in 1938, at the time of Munich, you preached sermons, which one can still read, that it was God's Holy Spirit which at that time guided and upheld the statesmen and made them strong (mark well, 'strong') for their 'struggle for peace' and for heavy and painful sacrifices (namely, the surrender of Czechoslovakia). Have not you, too, like every nation, the government you deserve? Now, in 1939, this government of yours could not be too loud in its protestations that the struggle in this war was one of 'foreign ideologies,' which did not touch you Swiss in the least. But nine months later, when things at first were going only too well for Hitler, and too badly for the others, your Foreign Minister delivered a speech in which he gave you the advice that it was time for you, too, to 'put on' the new man. I know that this Minister has gone now; but to this day no one knows whether the rest of your Federal Council was at that time of the same opinion or not. Your students at that time, not to mention your patriotically-minded students, conferred earnestly together whether a different Switzerland from the democracy of 1847 might not after all be feasible. If a man at that time publicly said that the

THE ONLY WAY

cause for which Britain had entered the war concerned the Swiss as well, then he was marked by the high-priests of your neutrality as having said something 'dangerous to the State.' Moreover, I have studied your great daily newspapers during these years, and I must confess that the way in which your leading articles and your correspondents have been guided by events has in general, and with honourable exceptions, given me an impression of complete senility. Then you set up a censorship which did not try to be a censorship. It withheld from you those expressions of opinion, and even those statements of facts, which were or might have been displeasing to our rulers. The decisions of this censorship conformed to the requirements of the situation; that is, the strictness or the mildness of its judgment could be fairly accurately inferred from a study of the map, in other words, from the state of the military fronts at the time. Meantime you were all the more keen to support, as long as you could, the efforts of our war industry with the well-known quality of your factories' work. And if, perhaps, that is to be explained and excused by looking at your geographical position, it still remains mysterious how in connection with this business you felt obliged to come to the help of the German war-effort with a round

THE ONLY WAY

milliard of good Swiss francs. Only after many a long day did you begin to take serious steps against your 'Frontists,'[1] and even then you gave your action a show of neutrality by undertaking a campaign at the same time against the Communists, from whom in these years you had notoriously nothing to fear. And in these same years it suited you—not the Swiss government this time, but a large number of Swiss townsfolk and peasants—to discover that you also did not really like the Jews and that it was a good time to pull a little in stroke with German anti-Semitism. This, and a few other things, are what I have gleaned of your attitude in these years.

"I see clearly that since last year everything looks different again, but I am certainly not wrong if I suppose that this has less to do with a change in your own opinions than with the altered 'situation.'

"Now if that was the statesman-like wisdom by which you thought to preserve your security and independence, that is your own affair. But I must say to you that—although and because I agree with your judgment in this matter—I do not understand rightly where you get the courage to confront us Germans from your present standpoint.

[1] Swiss Fascists.

THE ONLY WAY

You judge aright, but it seems to me that your judgment falls mostly heavily on your own heads. In the words of your National Anthem, 'Do we stand firm as rocks, not paling before danger?' No, as long as all went well with our Hitler you stood by no means firm as rocks; not there, where you now say you stand, did you care about another, better, free Germany, or raise your finger on behalf of it. But you cared for yourselves, you washed your hands in innocence, you played at impartiality and then, not once or twice, quite noticeably sided with the stronger party. About where Chamberlain's government stood in the time of Munich, about where the Vatican stood, about where the American isolationists stood till 1941, we have seen you standing the whole time. Where would you be today if things had gone on as they did up till 1941? Would the 'putting on of the new man' not have become a live option? And now you are concerned about us? Now you want to criticize us? Now you think you have something to say to us, to offer us, to give us, something profitable to hold out to us? No; you have not been the lighthouse in the midst of the breakers to which we could raise our eyes. What we saw was rather something like a weather-cock, moving neutrally but merrily. But we have seen enough of such weather-cocks in our own country, since 1933, and indeed long before that. All in all, what we heard from you were the words 'reasons of State.' With these very words on his lips, which are so truly atheistic, our Bismarck is said to have died. And so I am not so sure what use we Germans are to make of the sincere friendship which you, if all goes well, in such a praiseworthy manner want to extend to us.

"And how about Christianity in Switzerland? Is it true, what we have heard, that by Christianity you mean first the Gospel and then the Law? Can we be at all sure that the Christians in Switzerland will not meet us like a useless little army of self-righteous dogmatists? Do you Christians in Switzerland live by the grace of God in Jesus Christ, and will you be in a position to let us see something of that in a practical way? And if this is not the case, how do you mean to offer us sincere friendship in the other sense as well, of that unfaltering hardness which we need so badly? If all is not well with your own faith, how should you become worthy of our faith? In short, excuse my saying it, but it seems to me that you are all too obviously cut from the same cloth as we are.

"Understand me aright: I do not think that this excuses us. The universal night of sin in which all

THE ONLY WAY

cats are grey, in which none has anything to offer the other, is not the conclusion I wish to reach. I assure you again and again that you are in the right about us. But I fear that all the same you are not the people who are now able to give and to be something significant to us. I fear that your position is by no means so strong and powerful as it seems, for your approach to us (even if you make up your minds to it) to result in any great help for the salvation of Germany. I fear that democracy and Christianity as represented by you will not have on my wicked and foolish fellow-countrymen the overpowering effect of a heavenly message. You would have had to show throughout these past years a very different front in order to be justified and entitled to put the whole question raised in this pamphlet. And if I am not to lead you astray in the good resolutions which you will perhaps make along the lines you have indicated, then I must openly say to you, that I fear, for the reasons I have given, that it is not you who can do much here. I do not want to grieve you, my dear Swiss people, but it is possible that so far as we can be helped at all by men we shall have much more to receive and to learn from the Russians, for example, than from you."

So an educated German could speak, and I

THE ONLY WAY

must confess that I am not perfectly sure how I could answer him. I could, indeed, refer him to the firm words of Herr Obrecht of the Federal Council, in March, 1939, and to the unforgettable speech of our General on the Rütli; to the intrepid periodical *Nebelspalter* and to the *Cabaret Cornichon,* which cannot be too highly praised for the steadfastness of its message; to the "sound sense of the Swiss people," which was really maintained through everything, and a few times even directly and effectively aired its views in opposition to what came from Berne; to so many individuals who in these years have struggled might and main against the stream of government neutrality; to all kinds of private activities which have been pushed and driven and urged for the benefit, for example, of the refugees and the Jews; and above all, to the great instinctive matter-of-factness with which in the last resort the mass of our people and our army knew where they were, even when they did not dare to say it or let it be said aloud. I could refer to what friendly foreign journalists have now and again said in our favour at this time, and what we have gladly seen in print for our consolation. So far as the Church and Christianity are concerned, I could refer to the fact that the preaching in Switzerland, taken as a whole and on the average, is certainly better today—less moralistic and senti-

THE ONLY WAY

mental and, therefore, in the best sense, political and social—than it was twenty or forty years ago, and that in the congregations, too, amid all fluctuating opinions, there is a growing number of people who appreciate this improvement.

But we can see that all this would not suffice for a real and conclusive answer to what an educated German could ask us. The whole picture which is opposed to all this from the other side is too glaring. The official attitude of Switzerland—and this is unfortunately what counts—has certainly been in these years a very clever one, but unfortunately all in all it has been all too clever. We have behaved only as Swiss, we have proved ourselves to be good Swiss, but not good Europeans. Our reputation in the world has perhaps always been better than we ourselves have been in reality. We should not be surprised if after this war it has lost a little more of its ancient somewhat fairy-like glamour—to which the German Friedrich Schiller contributed something.

So it is a question whether we have the authority to give the Germans today what we owe them. It is no less a question because I have freely invented this educated German who could reproach us in this way. Who knows if he is only my invention, or if he does not already circulate in more than one copy, and can suddenly, at the given moment, meet us in reality and tell us to our face: "I question your authority"? But who could refute him, even if he existed only in my fancy? No, there it is: it is a question whether we Swiss really have the authority—so much so, that one might consider whether the theme, "The Germans and ourselves," were not better discarded, or dropped as speedily as possible, that we might turn with new thoroughness to the theme, "We Swiss."

We could do that. But we cannot escape in this way from the theme, "The Germans and ourselves"; certainly not today. The Germans are there, as the Jews are there, with whose nature and destiny they have so much in common. It is with the Germans, in fact, that we must come to some kind of understanding if we are really to be Swiss. The task of doing that properly remains even when we have to confess to ourselves that our authority in the matter is questionable. We can therefore retract nothing of what we have said, even after hearing what the educated German has to say.

It is a weird light into which at the end of the day we see that everything has moved. We do see now that we, too, when we think of those in the north are mounted on no gallant chargers, but on lowly asses with long ears, which do not lend

THE ONLY WAY

themselves to pomp. We do see that all open or hidden pride in Switzerland, with which we might have wished to face the Germans, has been crushed from the start through the fact that we are what we are. We certainly see that even the prayer, *God pity the Germans,* would be extremely inapposite unless it were based on the most heartfelt *Miserere nobis* and thus meant also *God pity us all.* And we do see that if, contrary to all human expectation, we were to carry out anything at all along the line we have discussed, then it would not be in virtue of our ability or achievement, and it would not be to our glory or triumph. We would, then, without our deserving it, and in our supremely questionable authority, be *used* for this work, as even a bad instrument can in certain circumstances be successfully used by a good workman. But we have no sort of claim even to be used in this way for this work. We could not be surprised if quite different people and nations than we were to be used for what the Germans need now.

But all this does not alter the fact that we are called today. That is what we should have to say in answer to the harshest critic of our authority, even if we could not answer one in a thousand of his objections. We must make no mistake about this. That we find we are not equal to the task does not release us. It must be assumed because it is laid upon us, not because we consider ourselves suited to carry it out. Our effort will not necessarily be fruitless. It will certainly not be fruitless so long as we make it in all humility. What matters is our attitude to those who can have a future only by beginning from zero. And we for our part must likewise begin from zero, that we may be able to stand by them in this situation. If we have to bend low that is no bad beginning, but a good one, perhaps the only possible one, for standing by those who are laid so low.

For them as for us, then, for their own future way as for ours in relation to them, everything depends on this—that no one is bowed down by a sorrow that worketh death and not life, that in reality the eternal mercy of our Creator and Saviour—Jesus Christ in person, the true "Lord of history"—illuminates, and is mighty and victorious at that very zero point, and that it is given to them and to us to meet the hopelessness of their situation, and our questionable authority in relation to them, with the mightiest of all prayers, "Lord I believe: help thou mine unbelief." Then we can and we shall come together—and not in vain—the Germans and ourselves. He who makes this his concern will not be deterred at our theme being revealed in the end in an uncanny and somewhat sinister light.